MW00423128

# THE POWER OF
# Goal ZERO

### Results Focused Leadership for Achieving Superior Performance

Robert,

Your leadership is taking Axalta to new heights. Let's enjoy the ride. Keep driving for excellence.

Best Regards, Sam

**Sam Smolik** 8-20-21

# Endorsements (Condensed)

"Safety performance is about leadership, culture, processes, and discipline. Sam's passion for safety really comes through in this book."
**– Bob Patel, Chief Executive Officer, Lyondellbasell Industries**

"This book is a must read for anyone seeking to take his/her organization to the next level of performance and competitive differentiation!"
**– Robert W. Bryant, Chief Executive Officer, Axalta Coating Systems**

"Sam's book accomplishes what hundreds of other publications have attempted to do, which is to simplify and clearly state how to achieve step change in an organization."
**– Charlie Shaver, Chairman and CEO, Nouryon Chemicals (Carlyle Private Equity)**

"Sam Smolik was my very first management new hire at LyondellBasell after I was brought in to help the company recover and emerge from bankruptcy. Our employees led the way with best-in-class operational performance, cost structure and most importantly, industry leading safety results."
**– James Gallogly, Former Chief Executive Officer, LyondellBasell**

"This book offers a comprehensive step-by-step approach to creating an incident and injury free workplace. A must read for today's managers."
**– Jeet Bindra, Retired President, Chevron Global Manufacturing**

"When you invest 50 years of your life into something with the passion and skill of Sam Smolik, amazing things happen. Businesses have been improved and transformed, people have been changed, and most importantly, through his focus on safety, lives have been saved."
**– Kevin Garland, Chief Executive Officer, Mountaire Farms**

"The Power of Goal ZERO is strong because it is real event driven with truthful outcomes."
**– Jon Hodges, Founder and CEO, Evergreen North America**

"Sam Smolik's decades of experience make this book a must read for anyone who wants a roadmap to safety excellence."
**– Katie Mehnert, Chief Executive Officer, ALLY Energy**

"Sam's passion for leading people leaps off the page and is a powerful, contagious lesson."
**– Chet Thompson, President & CEO, American Fuel & Petrochemical Manufacturers (AFPM)**

"This Opus demonstrates Smolik's lifetime commitment to the industry and unveils an inspiring legacy to the young generation of Leaders for Excellence."
**– William Garcia, Executive Director, Cefic, The European Chemicals Industry Council**

"I wish The Power of Goal ZERO had been available and part of the required reading list when I was in business school."
**– Rogers Hoyt, Jr., Chairman of the Board, Ducks Unlimited, Inc.**

"Sam Smolik is the ideal author of this definitive book on Goal ZERO. His book is destined to be a best seller."
**– George Pilko, Founder and Chairman, Pilko & Associates**

"Leaders at all levels can benefit from Sam's experiences and suggestions."
**– Phil Hawk, former Chairman and Chief Executive Officer, TEAM, Inc.**

"I am comfortable concluding that Sam's book is the most comprehensive on the subject of Operational Excellence—from the tactics and anecdotes for leaders to the strategies and philosophies behind the best management systems in industry today."
**– Joe Stough, Founder and Former Chief Executive Officer of Syntex**

"For many readers, this is an opportunity to benefit from an industry executive that you never had the chance to interview."
– **David Zimmerman, PE and Former Group President, KBR, Inc.**

"Informed by a 50-year career of leadership experience with some of the world's most recognized and admired manufacturing companies, Sam has captured the essence of how strong and empathetic leadership can drive sustainable business performance to the highest levels. Sam gets it!"
– **Don A. Young, Executive Vice President of EHS & Sustainability, J.M. Huber Corporation**

"The Power of Goal Zero offers valuable lessons for business majors who want to launch, manage, or work in successful companies; therefore, I believe it should be required reading in business schools around the country."
– **Marianne Gooch, President, DynaComm**

"Sam's fun stories, simple wisdoms, and insightful perspective will change the way you think, and will improve your organization's performance."
– **Dustin Olson, Chief Manufacturing Officer, Purecycle Technologies**

As a Safety & Health professional, the Goal ZERO transformation was one of the most exciting and rewarding experiences of my career."
– **Cynthia Childs, CSP/CIH (retired), Former Americas HSE Director, LyondellBasell**

**READ FULL ENDORSEMENTS - PAGE 233**

# THE POWER OF
# Goal ZERO

## *Results Focused Leadership for Achieving Superior Performance*

## Sam Smolik

Names: Smolik, Sam, author

Title: *The Power of Goal ZERO*: Results Focused Leadership for Achieving Superior Performance / Sam Smolik

Library of Congress Control Number: 2021907783

ISBN:        978-1-7364585-0-1 Hardcover
             978-1-7364585-1-8 Paperback
             978-1-7364585-2-5 eBook


Quality First Publishing
Houston, TX 77056

Book design by Brett Carr, Kodiack Studios.

# CONTENTS

# Acknowledgments

This book is dedicated to the thousands of people that I worked with throughout my career. I was fortunate to work in three highly reputable companies and with inspirational people all around the world. I worked with many fine people in industry associations for the betterment of the industry as a whole. I traveled the world extensively, meeting new people everywhere I ventured to. I constantly tried to provide collaborative leadership and encouragement while marveling at how well people responded, came together as a team, and came up with creative ideas.

As I was approaching retirement from LyondellBasell, I commissioned a global team to help build out my comprehensive vision for taking Operational Excellence to the next level. We called the program Technology and Knowledge Management (TKM) and focused on a balanced and integrated approach to Leadership, People, Culture, Systems, and Assets. I want to acknowledge the team members: Giorgio Bagni, Rick Beleutz, Shane Fandry, Jean Gadbois, Jim Hillier, Eric Mesle, Tom Myers, Dustin Olson, Patricia Shieh-Lance, and Edwin Stotefalk.

I also want to thank my many colleagues and friends that read the drafts of my book and provided invaluable feedback for improvement: Mark Cluff, Bill Cook, Brian Cook, Rebecca Corbin, John Evans, William Garcia, Jean Gadbois, Marianne Gooch, Brett Hafer, Phil Hawk, Jon Hodges, Gary Jones, Julie Lautens, Mike McCandless, Mike McGinnis, Katie Mehnert, Tom Myers, Dustin Olson, Laurence Pearlman, Bruce Piasecki, George Pilko, Jan Pilko, Alex Pollock, Emily Boykin Poole, Lara Swett, Joe Stough, Bert Visser, Peter Webb, and David Zimmerman. Each of you helped to make the book better, and I am extremely grateful.

Finally, I couldn't have written this book without the support of my terrific wife Stephanie. We've been married for 47 years and she has been my rock. She has been supportive and patient with my many hours of writing just as she has been throughout my entire career. We are a true partnership.

# Foreword

by Bruce Piasecki, AHC Group President and Founder and
New York Times bestselling author

**Summary:** Sam Smolik has offered a book of significant corporate and social impact. Thirty years from now, in returning to your shelves at office or home, you might say: "I am glad I came across this life summary in 2021." The hashtags of this book include leadership, operational excellence, global firms, competition, and I'd add "compassionate management styles."

**Background:** I have benefited from knowing Sam since he first worked as a top executive at Dow, when my firm was young. More than thirty years later, Sam Smolik's advice has crystalized in this book. Back about a decade, I knew Sam when he was major senior executive at Shell, where we'd visit him at ONE SHELL PLAZA, in the skyrise. He was kind and compassionate and giving then, too. He has always been generous with his time, a fine mentor. And when it came to writing a book, he reached out to me, so the roles switched for a bit. And now we have this fine book before us.

**Timing of this Book:** This gifted articulate former executive has taught us how to protect the wealth of a global firm with wit, focus, and discipline. After the tragedies at so many failed enterprises—from Volkswagen's emissions scandals to the fraudulent claims of bribery and wrongdoing in other firms—it pays to invest the time to read up and reflect on this life of positive lessons in management. Risk enterprise systems, and the power of gaining leverage over Goal ZERO protocols, are the name of the game today, from Walmart and Unilever to the many smaller firms supplying a world of giants.

In this readable book, Sam gives you a game plan worth delivering on.

**Why This Book is Consequential in Business and Society Today**

As more and more firms go global, with complex risk enterprise systems, the executives running these firms encounter, every day, new and lasting forms of competitive advantage and significant risk. I've called this management decision-making "in a swift and severe world."

In fact, I am certain that many social ills can only be improved through better corporate management of risks—from poverty to pandemics to social unrest. You see that even this week of April 2021, when CEOs, more than 100 of them, are talking about the need to protect proper voting rights! This is what I called "social response capitalism" in my book World Inc. Sam has taken the concept and operationalized it, internalized all this into how a global firm must operate.

Ignoring Sam's advice comes at a cost, coast to coast. You can run into a wall faster than ever before or begin an ascent of magnifying consequences. Everything is faster and more furious in a sense; but getting the systems right in the first-place matter more than ever. In between these two goal posts of prevention and performance, you will find survival, failure, and the accumulation of great wealth. Sam Smolik's career and work is about finding that exact middle, the sweet spot of Operational Excellence. Goal Zero is the new generation code word.

In this book before you—a smart book—Sam has written an available, well-researched, and important summary of how to enhance the performance of your organization. You can think of this as a sustained tutorial you will never forget. He even starts from his early Boy Scout experiences, and those as a quarterback on his high football team. There is a down-home sportiveness to his earnest portrayal of what works. This is not a dry book, but full of nutrition for the aspiring manager and executive.

Academic thinkers called the transformation to these higher performance standards "good to great" (Jim Collins), or "re-engineering" your firm. Those frames only take you so far, into the realm of the aspirational. Smolik takes you over the goal line. The voice in this book is valid, authentic, and of consequence. It does not surprise me to learn that Sam Smolik—

after Dow, Shell and LyondellBasell—serves on corporate boards. We are all lucky he has now taken the time to write this book based on so much experience doing.

## How He Learned to Make the Complex Simple Again

Sam learned his lessons from being a Vice President of Environment, Health and Safety at Dow global, then Shell International, and finally at LyondellBasell. Each stage of his career becomes a springboard for intelligent narratives about what works and what does not in managing complex organizations. It is fun to collect these asides and tales, along with the larger argument.

*The Power of Goal ZERO* is a master's guidebook on how to achieve superior performance in every sense of the phrase "achieving results." What do you think about when you think of mastery? I can see Sam passing efficient spirals, making the right moves for short-yard gains, and the long-term wins. Mastery is about achieving results even in the thorny and the rough and the tumble. He thinks on his feet in this book but always with sound principles and steady footing in fact and management experience. He will teach you how to be adept in the short run and adaptive in the long.

The key components of this book are available for your reflection in the Table of Contents. View its intelligence as one found in the best-designed menus. You have a feast of options before you; but Sam makes the sequence of what to learn digestible and actionable. Read this book from start to finish, as I have in its early drafts to this complete formulation.

## Preventing Something from Going Wrong

Sustainable organizations require a great deal of effort. As Sam aptly notes, this effort must be sustained with "a passion for leadership and people." The sequence of chapters from chapter three to six are perhaps the most precious, and the ones not to overlook. It is a happy day when a book like this comes out; as it helps us all have faith in the future, and look around the corner of our firms with wealth, result, and satisfaction before us.

While it is accurate to say the bulk of this book is about preventing something from going wrong, it is much about what is right. You get the feeling of this in a passage on balance, where Sam talks about how he coached his son's baseball team for nine years, despite all his other obligations. He writes, and I quote:

"Colin Powell is an American politician, diplomat and retired four-star general who serves as the 65th United States Secretary of State. He summed it (balance) up nicely when he said: 'Have fun in your command. Don't always run at breakneck speed. Take leave when you've earned it; spend time with your families. Corollary: surround yourself with people who take their work seriously, but not themselves, those who work hard and play hard.'"

You can see these values and principles in this life work of Sam Smolik. I trust you will benefit from reading this book and enjoy and cherish it as much as I have.

# Introduction

*The Power of Goal ZERO* serves as a "virtual mentor" for leaders and aspiring leaders at all levels to improve personal effectiveness, organizational efficiency, and motivation of people. The principles enable rapid transformation in any organization. Through personal stories and experiences, a proven roadmap is provided for demonstrating strong leadership, creating a culture of excellence, implementing organizational change, developing effective management systems, and achieving superior performance. In today's competitive environment, individuals and organizations must be best in class to compete and win.

The book is a condensed version of successful techniques learned in a 50-year career of driving improvement in multinational organizations. It describes a practical way to be a results focused leader and drive safety, reliability, and quality improvement. The book has value for people in any type of organization regardless of the product produced or service provided. Leadership and organizational concepts are universal. Beginning employees, front line supervisors, mid-level leaders, department managers, C-Suite executives, small business owners, and CEOs can all benefit. Young people beginning their careers are my personal target since I've always had a passion for coaching and mentoring new employees.

Thousands of management and leadership books have been written. Why is this one any different? *All* of the examples presented in this book are not idle theories; they have all been tested and proven by my colleagues and me in major global corporations. This book summarizes the best practices in a manner that readers can easily understand and implement.

An incredible number of factors are important for an organization to win. It's helpful to break these down into reasonable and understandable components to ensure the path to excellence in performance becomes clear for all and to help with focus. Throughout the book, I'll provide tips for each of the following elements in my formula for achieving Operational Excellence. I use the term **Operational Excellenc**e based on my manufacturing background and it works in any type of organization.

## Operational Excellence =
## Leadership + People + Culture + Systems + Assets

I'm not aware of many books that deal with these five topics in an integrated manner for achieving Operational Excellence. I saw a void and felt compelled to share the valuable lessons that we have learned in this space. We created a system in which each of these items are interdependent and yield significant results if performed together in a systematic manner. We will discuss each of these focus areas and demonstrate how they collectively will lead your organization to achieve excellence in performance.

The principles apply to any type of organization—manufacturing, construction, or service industry. To win in any organization, you must be the best and strive for excellence in safety, profitability, reliability, quality, efficiency, consistency, cost management and customer satisfaction as well as environment, social, and governance (ESG) objectives—*all of these*. Excellence in performance for all areas of an organization may sound overwhelming, right? But it doesn't have to be; keep the approach well organized and clear for all.

The concept of Operational Excellence provides an umbrella approach to these objectives and an associated management system provides the structure for how work gets done. A good management system and a Goal ZERO culture provide a foundation of discipline in the organization. The result is a strong, consistent platform for conducting work, building on best practices, and accelerating performance improvement. Strict prioritization and simplicity are critical to avoid the constraints and performance drags that overly prescriptive systems create. Your primary goal should be to achieve Operational Excellence in *everything* you and the people in your organization do.

Operational Excellence is not a sexy or exciting subject. It doesn't get the attention it deserves in many organizations *until performance declines, or something goes extremely wrong*. It's similar in our homes. We take for granted a good supply of running water or electricity until we don't have it; then it becomes urgent.

Leaders like to focus on the items that create the most excitement: growth, innovation, technology development, mergers, and acquisitions (M&A), ESG progress, and creating shareholder value—and so do I. I contend, however, that you will never be successful in any of these areas and achieve superior performance if you don't have a solid foundation and constant daily pursuit of Operational Excellence. I provide an outline and suggestions for how to achieve and maintain excellence with the basics of business which then allows greater progress on your loftier objectives. A consistent program for risk management is essential in today's world. You can't talk credibly about societal progress while at the same time hurting people and negatively impacting the environment.

We all know success in any organization begins with strong leadership. Results focused leaders understand human factors and how to motivate people to achieve more than they ever imagined. Great leaders consistently create and articulate a compelling vision—a better place where people aspire to reach. A major portion of the book discusses the subject of leadership and human behavior management. It's extremely rewarding to create a consistent culture of competence, confidence, capability, ownership, responsibility, attention to detail, pride, and winning.

In the book, I describe the concept of Goal ZERO. It's a foundational leadership tool that has an enormous impact across the entire organization. Goal ZERO helps create a culture of discipline and is easy for people to understand. Here's a quick description to help you connect the dots throughout the book:

*Goal ZERO serves as a foundation for a **culture** of doing things the right way, every day. It creates high level expectations for **leadership** and **people** as they drive towards and achieve **Operational Excellence.***

By the end of the book, you'll be able to answer the question, "What is Goal ZERO?" Goal ZERO is such a strong, positive aspect of a winning culture that I have used it in the title of the book. Goal ZERO is actionable and impacts every individual in an organization. It's a relentless focus on the basic building blocks of excellence: ZERO defects, ZERO rule breaking, ZERO unsafe acts, ZERO non-compliance, ZERO incidents, and ZERO missed value creating opportunities. Goal ZERO serves as a "north star" for your team in driving for excellence. It becomes a global code word for "doing the right thing at all times."

Vitally important, Goal ZERO is about compassion and caring for your people. Goal ZERO performance, Goal ZERO behavior, etc. are all terms you will hear from your people. It's a way to express your combined expectations and values in one term. A Goal ZERO mentality is powerful and provides simple clarity of expectations across the entire organization. Goal ZERO becomes a way of life for an everyday approach to safety, reliability, quality, and everything else.

A good **system** and the importance of properly maintaining **assets** are vitally important. Systems describe "how things are done around here" and can include items such as technology, best practices, requirements, procedures, and work processes. Many organizations have some type of management system, but the system is often out of date, too bureaucratic, and not always followed. Lack of a functioning system introduces unnecessary variation into the organization, creating conditions for undesired results and lost value creating opportunities. Leadership is about creating a consistent system that drives change, unleashes the power of people, and delivers continuous improvement. While leaders have many types of personal styles, all good leaders utilize a systems approach to help achieve their objectives.

Most young people entering the workforce don't understand management systems and the importance of compliance with standard requirements. Most requirements have been developed following significant incidents in the past resulting in loss of life, property damage, business interruption, or significant customer impacts. New employees typically learn the importance once they experience or witness a devasting incident themselves, but then it's too late. Reading this book will help you gain a clear understanding of the importance of a time-tested management system and develop a proactive sense of urgency for compliance and defect-free behavior.

The book covers topics for unlocking your full potential, strengthening your leadership skills, and motivating people in your organization to achieve more than they ever imagined. I lay out a clear roadmap for how to design, utilize, and maintain a good management system that will increase an organization's performance and productivity. Simplicity is a prevailing theme; it doesn't have to be complicated.

Many companies waste too much time trying to determine "what" went wrong and "how" to drive performance improvement. The same frustrating mistakes get repeated over and over again. This book illustrates the methods for documenting the "how" into a management system so you can then focus the majority of your efforts on "execution and implementation." A corporate strategy is worthless if you don't execute well.

The principles in this book will provide clear guidance for how information can be organized and what is needed for success. A management system will provide clarity and take churn out of the organization. A good management system gives people the confidence to know they are on the right track, the courage to drive harder and the tools needed to win.

I use "safety" as an example or metaphor throughout the book. You must never allow anyone to get seriously injured in your organization. A serious injury impacts everyone: the injured person, family, friends, and co-workers in the organization. "Nothing is more important than the safety of our employees, customers, and the public." You hear this quite often in the industry. Some leaders just say it; others live it every day.

A key message of the book is that the pre-conditions for achieving excellence in safety are the same as for achieving excellence in your operations. You need strong leadership, competent people operating flawlessly, a winning culture, a good management system, solid technology, and well-maintained assets. When you have each of these, you will not only achieve superior safety performance, but you will also reduce defects, increase reliability, lower costs, improve consistency of your products, enhance the customer experience, and drive value to the bottom line. It makes perfect sense to passionately lead with safety. Leading with safety protects people and also helps to achieve the other objectives important to your organization.

I spent my career with three leading international companies: LyondellBasell Industries, Royal Dutch Shell, and

Dow Chemical. I served as Global Vice President for each of these companies in a variety of Environment, Health, Safety, Security, Operational Excellence, Sustainable Development, and Manufacturing roles. During these years, I participated in literally thousands of engagements with people (both internal and external to my companies) on the elements that contribute to Operational Excellence. I had the privilege to work with many outstanding and smart CEOs, business leaders, operations leaders, environment, health, and safety (EH&S) professionals, and front-line personnel. There are far too many to name individually. Many creative people populate our world, and I was extremely fortunate to be associated with many of them.

Throughout my career, I took every opportunity I could to learn from more experienced people. I was privileged to meet the famous W. Edwards Deming and attend his conference in 1988. Deming was an American engineer, statistician, professor, author, lecturer, and management consultant. He is best known for his work driving quality improvement in Japan following World War II. I always believed in the saying, "Most knowledge is gained at the foot of the elderly." Deming referred to it as "divine knowledge."

I retired from LyondellBasell as Senior Vice President, Americas Manufacturing, in 2017. LyondellBasell is one of the world's largest petrochemical companies. I joined LyondellBasell in 2009 after the company had filed for bankruptcy earlier that year. Our corporate leadership team and each of our global employees worked long hours and endless weekends to bring the company out of bankruptcy and transform the company into one of the safest, most reliable, and lowest-cost producers in the industry. The Goal ZERO and Operational Excellence approach was a significant factor in the success of the company.

LyondellBasell won the American Chemistry Council Responsible Care® Company of the Year Award in 2014 and again in 2020. This award is presented annually to the best company in the industry for innovative practices and leadership in the areas of environment, health, safety, and security. Goal ZERO and Operational Excellence provide a sustainable, competitive advantage that LyondellBasell has achieved and continues to enjoy today. I am proud to share some of our proven concepts for the benefit of helping other companies protect their people and improve efficiency.

Years ago, my good friend Bruce Piasecki, President and Founder of the AHC Group, Inc., invited me to New York for one of his industry conferences. He asked me to present the learnings from my years of experience. As I was preparing for the talk, I listened to a well-versed song by Tracy Lawrence, "Lessons Learned." One verse is so true for all of us:

*Lessons learned, they sure run deep,*
*They don't go away, and they don't come cheap.*
*There's no way around it,*
*This world turns......on lessons learned.*

The lyrics in this song are powerful. Lessons are, unfortunately, learned the hard way and the memories stick with us. They sure don't come cheap in energy and petrochemical industries with fires, explosions, environmental damage, injuries, and even fatalities. We often say there aren't many new types of root causes to incidents, just repeats of the same old mistakes. The challenge is in how to capture these lessons and embed them into the everyday work practices and culture of a company.

My approach in the book is to illustrate key concepts in short, practical sections. I utilize personal stories and anecdotes to illustrate the context and provide examples of how you, too, can drive towards Operational Excellence at any level. Imagine yourself in a similar situation when you read my stories. Many of my comments are targeted at senior leaders but the lessons are appropriate for people at any level. Demonstrating leadership and providing a sense of ownership for individuals at all levels are important elements for success.

I write this book with great humility because many of you could have written it. I certainly don't want to give the impression that I have all the answers, or that my recommendations are the only way to conduct your business. I am simply sharing these life lessons that have come from the school of hard knocks. I made many mistakes along the way and learned from each one. You may not agree with some of my recommendations and that's okay; diversity of thought is good.

I openly share my stories and experiences in the spirit of learning and improving, especially for young people. I use "we" throughout the book to describe examples because I worked with terrific teams at my companies, and we developed the processes together and drove results. I'll also admit that I learned a lot while writing this book as I researched deeper into a few of the topics that I cover. Hopefully, you will use this book as one of your key references and as a virtual mentor throughout your career.

I have read many books on leadership and organizational effectiveness throughout my career. I always felt if I learned one or two tips, then it was worth my time buying and reading the book. I've tried to provide you with the same opportunity in this book. I guarantee you will take away more than one or two tips and best practices that you can implement immediately.

# CHAPTER 1

## The Goal ZERO Approach

During my 50-year career, I've researched and observed numerous programs, slogans, themes, and approaches to safety and achieving excellence. Nothing comes close to the effectiveness of Goal ZERO. This chapter covers the philosophy behind Goal ZERO and how it is such a powerful force in helping to create a winning culture. Simply put, Goal ZERO is a driver for achieving **excellence** in any organization, and performance **excellence** contributes to top-notch value creation and risk management.

I will blend in personal stories dealing with the Goal ZERO impact on safety, but the Goal ZERO concept impacts all areas of performance and excellence. In this chapter, I explain *The Power of Goal ZERO* and what it means to be a Goal ZERO company. An emphasis on continuous improvement may be good, but to achieve a paradigm shift in performance, a culture of ZERO sends a clearer, absolute message. ZERO means having a positive, proactive culture of excellence in which you expect ZERO defects, ZERO rule breaking, ZERO non-compliance, ZERO incidents, and ZERO missed value creating opportunities.

A considerable number of companies use terms for the Goal ZERO concept such as Target ZERO, Mission ZERO, ZERO Harm, Safety First, No One Gets Hurt, etc. You can also choose a non-safety theme such as Excellence Every Day, Striving for Perfection, or Driving Perfect Performance. These terms are all good. The point is the theme should be **memorable, actionable, and become ingrained in everyone's minds daily.** Pick one that works for your company and stick with it.

**GOAL ZERO NUGGET:**
*Choose a Goal ZERO theme that's*
*actionable and memorable.*

# Goal ZERO—An Overview

Goal ZERO is not complicated, but it is powerful. Simple things are always better. Goal ZERO is an easy-to-understand expectation of excellence in everything that you do; continuous improvement isn't good enough anymore. It's a human factor cultural change tool that works across any company and in any industry. Goal ZERO creates a culture of discipline. It's a belief that every one of us can work defect-free, every day. Achieving Operational Excellence takes dedicated leadership and a Goal ZERO approach with respect to people, culture, systems, and assets to achieve desired results in safety, reliability, and quality.

Goal ZERO has many meanings and is used commonly in an organization's vocabulary. First, Goal ZERO is a noun. Examples are: "We work hard to achieve Goal ZERO," "Goal ZERO is a foundation for excellence," "Goal ZERO impacts every person in the organization," and "Goal ZERO becomes a way of life."

Goal ZERO is also an adjective. Examples are: "We are a Goal ZERO company," "The Goal ZERO culture in our company guides behavior," "People appreciate working for a Goal ZERO company," and "Following rules and paying attention to detail are signs of Goal ZERO performance."

One of the most important factors in the success of establishing a Goal ZERO organization is leadership alignment. Once leaders and employees in the organization begin to truly understand the concept, they become enthusiastic supporters. Goal ZERO is the right thing to do. Goal ZERO helps protect people, it reduces defects in people's work as well as being beneficial for business. Leading with safety is an intuitive way to introduce Goal ZERO and then expand into all areas of Operational Excellence.

We first introduced Goal ZERO at Shell worldwide in 2007. I give credit to my friend Paul Tebo for triggering our thoughts around this concept. Paul had a successful career at DuPont, with his last assignment as Corporate Vice President for Health, Safety, and Environment. As I began to understand the Goal ZERO concept, I became a believer and enthusiastic supporter.

On my first day at LyondellBasell in 2009, I didn't waste any time and introduced Goal ZERO with a single slide (Figure 1).

# Goal ZERO

- Simple Phrase – major mindset shift
- Believing and Expecting
  - ZERO injuries
  - ZERO incidents
  - ZERO unsafe acts
  - ZERO defects
- Personalize it

FIGURE 1

The initial focus was on safety, but the overall intention from the beginning was to achieve Operational Excellence in everything we did. I firmly stated that we were going to change the culture into one that expects ZERO injuries, ZERO reliability incidents, ZERO quality incidents, ZERO non-compliance, and ZERO defects. Nominal yearly improvement was no longer good enough. As you can imagine, many people thought such a goal was unachievable.

What ensued was a considerable amount of discussion at all levels in the organization which I enjoyed very much. People need some time to think about the concept of Goal ZERO and internalize what it actually means. This discussion process is healthy and builds long term commitment. As leadership and our people began to endorse the concept, Goal ZERO became a foundational element of the culture of our company.

In the beginning, I heard over and over that Goal ZERO wasn't possible, "It's impossible for such a large company to have ZERO incidents." However, that wasn't the point at all. ZERO is possible for each of us individually on any given task. Goal ZERO is not about the company as a whole, it's about you and me individually, task by task. For example, if each person works each day incident free, the entire company will work incident free, one day at a time. It's amazing how quickly the concept catches on as people begin to internalize and personalize it. It's about protecting people.

Undoubtedly, Goal ZERO changes the entire mindset of every person in the organization. People start to realize that we expect every person to perform to Goal ZERO expectations every day, on everything they do.

> **GOAL ZERO NUGGET:**
> *Goal ZERO is achievable for each*
> *one of us individually.*

# Proven Performance Results

Here's an example of safety metrics to illustrate the impact of Goal ZERO. The Occupational Safety and Health Administration (OSHA) provides oversight for safety performance in the United States. The metric for personal injury and illness rate is *incidents per 200,000 work hours.* An easier way to think about it is injuries in a year per 100 workers. A 1.0 OSHA rate is approximately equivalent to *1 injury for every 100 workers.* Figure 2 shows the average OSHA injury/illness rates for various industries in the year 2019.

| OSHA RECORDABLE INJURY and ILLNESS RATES | 2019 |
|---|---|
| Agriculture and Forestry | 5.2 |
| Transportation and Warehousing | 4.4 |
| Arts, Entertainment, and Recreation | 4.0 |
| Health Care | 3.8 |
| Manufacturing | 3.3 |
| Construction | 2.8 |
| Utilities | 2.2 |
| Petrochemicals | 0.73 |
| *Injuries per 200,000 work hours* *Approximate annual injuries per 100 workers* | |

FIGURE 2
Sources: Bureau of Labor statistics—US Department of Labor and American Chemistry Council (ACC)

Note that the petrochemical industry has an extremely low injury/illness rate. I attribute this statistic to the constant focus on safety by industry leaders over many years. A company in the energy and petrochemical industry can't be great if it doesn't have superior safety performance, which is true for many other industries as well. A major incident or serious noncompliance can have devastating consequences in loss of life, brand damage, litigation, and employee morale. No leader ever wants to make the call to a family member of a person that has lost his or her life in an accident.

Our expectation in LyondellBasell was to be the best at protecting people. With a Goal ZERO approach, we achieved a recordable rate at LyondellBasell for our combined workforce (employees and contractors) of approximately 0.20 on a consistent annual basis (that's one OSHA recordable injury annually for every 500 workers). That number is in the top decile of one of the best performing industries—the best of the best. We were recognized consistently by the American Chemistry Council (ACC) and the American Fuels and Petrochemical Industries (AFPM) as one the safest companies in the industry. And an added benefit, the reliability of our operating plants improved considerably. We were all extremely proud of these achievements and worked hard at them daily.

# Making Goal ZERO Personal

Goal ZERO performance in safety is indeed possible for each of us individually. If my good friend Cindy has one injury in 100 years of working, her personal recordable rate will be 1.0. Of course, no one works 100 years, so if she has only one injury in a 40-year career, her personal recordable rate will be 2.50—still way above the industry norm. For Cindy's personal OSHA rate to meet LyondellBasell standards of 0.20, she will have to work *500 years* with only one injury. Think about it.

As these numbers begin to sink in, people start to personalize Goal ZERO and realize that the vast majority of workers never get hurt. You can and should never get hurt—that's the fundamental belief of Goal ZERO. *But safety is not about the numbers;* safety is about the overall protection of people. It's about saving lives. The consequences of any injury can be life changing.

We conducted countless numbers of Goal ZERO Culture Workshops for our employees and contractors to help them internalize the concepts of Goal ZERO. JMJ Associates worked with us to develop the initial workshops and then our Global Safety Director Gary Jones and his team led the facilitation efforts around the LyondellBasell world.

These workshops turned out to be life-changing events for our people. Rather than specifically defining Goal ZERO, we used a variety of videos, stories, and examples of serious incidents to introduce topics. One of the most effective videos was called "Remember Charlie." It's the story of Charlie Morecraft's near death experience in a refinery explosion. He tells the story passionately and describes how taking a shortcut and breaking some rules changed his life forever. It's a well done, emotional video that is certain to get your attention.

Our approach in the workshops was to facilitate discussions and lead the people rather than tell them what to do. We'd ask people to think deeply about the consequences of a serious injury and what it would be like for their family if they didn't make it home from work. We used small group breakout sessions for discussion on why Goal ZERO behavior was so important and what it meant to them.

As we gathered back together, individuals gave emotional testimonies of their experiences. At times, people cried as they talked about the impact a serious injury would have on their loved ones. Imagine never getting to play baseball with your son again or never getting to watch your daughter's dance recital. Time and time again, people said they thought they had been working safely but now realized they had been nonchalant about it. Goal ZERO took them to an entirely new level and made them much more proactive in their work to prevent incidents and defects. We used the powerful theme, **"Goal ZERO begins with me."**

Over time, we developed a toolbox of additional workshops and tools that all centered around the Goal ZERO theme. Coaching to Goal ZERO was one of the more popular ones for helping front-line supervisors.

There were many keys to success for these workshops. The workshops were led by our internal staff and we engaged local people from the host location to help with the facilitation, especially when breaking into small groups. Cultures varied from country to country, so patience was necessary to give time for concepts to be understood and internalized. Translating materials into the local language was critical. Before we left a site, we wanted the local people to understand Goal ZERO, believe in Goal ZERO, and own Goal ZERO.

People are smart and can accept principles if they understand "why" the principles are important and have some data to back them up. People begin to change their belief about Goal ZERO and that not getting hurt is indeed possible and expected. They know and believe they can achieve Goal ZERO and expect everyone around them to do the same. People recognize that by risking incident and injury, they are putting everyone they care for in jeopardy. If each person accomplishes each task, every day, injury free, they will make it injury free the entire year.

Team members begin to understand that the only way to achieve Goal ZERO is to follow the rules at all times (even when no one is watching), to do a good pre-task analysis before each task to think about the hazards and precautions to take, and to focus on the task from start to finish. By focusing on incident prevention, the mistakes affecting quality and reliability also dramatically decrease.

Within a short time, as Goal ZERO catches on, you can see the passion in people as they begin to personally understand the concept. Injury rates rapidly decrease and so do plant operational incidents. Reliability improves and quality incidents occur much less frequently. A Goal ZERO culture impacts everything throughout the organization. People begin promoting and explaining Goal ZERO to others. They work with a Goal ZERO attitude because they want to, not because they have to. As time progressed, I always felt an enormous sense of accomplishment when visiting our plants around the world and listening to the people tell me what Goal ZERO meant to them—in many different languages. Goal ZERO catches on like wildfire and changes the company.

> ***GOAL ZERO NUGGET:***
> *Personalize safety and Goal ZERO.*

# Goal ZERO for Contractors

Contractors are a vital component for success in a manufacturing organization. Contractors tend to perform many of the higher risk activities, so Goal ZERO is especially important for them. Our employees articulated Goal ZERO expectations to every contractor as soon as he/she set a foot our property. Our employees and contractors were both proud to be working in a Goal ZERO company that cared so much for their safety.

One of our success factors was an annual conference we conducted with the CEOs of our largest contractor companies. The purpose was to establish strong relations at the top, to align on expectations and to share best practices. The CEOs of these companies were smart individuals with enormous experience. We all improved by working together. We wanted each of our contractor employees to work with the same Goal ZERO spirit as our own employees.

The contractor CEOs understood that we would only work with the safest contractor companies. In return, the safest companies would secure the most business. At that time, the average contractor OSHA rate in our industry was around 1.60. The companies that we selected to do business with averaged an OSHA rate of 0.60. And what's even better, these companies maintained an average 0.20 rate when working in our facilities—the same as our employees. In other words, we selected the safest contractor companies available, and they performed even better when working with us. Everyone knew the expectations of Goal ZERO, and they delivered!

# A Word of Caution

Now that I have explained the virtues of a Goal ZERO approach, I want to issue a word of caution. Goal ZERO, by itself, is not a safety program. Instead, it's a platform on which to build a culture of excellence in safety and everything else. A very poor example sometimes seen in companies is to employ a very simplistic ZERO-harm safety approach. I've witnessed this tactic in some contractor organizations that negotiate a safety incentive award as part of their contract for the work. For each month that the employees work injury free, they receive an award. If someone gets injured during the month, no one receives an award that month. To make matters worse, if an employee gets injured, he or she gets singled out for causing everyone else to lose their reward.

Of course, if this ZERO-harm safety approach is the full extent of a company's safety program, it's a terrible approach. This approach will lead to all types of unintended consequences. People will hide injuries, not report near misses and the organization will never learn and improve. If this approach is your intention with Goal ZERO, forget it...... *and never tell anyone that you read my book!*

The key to Goal ZERO is to set clear expectations and then focus on the positive. ZERO is very easy for people to understand and becomes a motivating factor. The purpose of this book is to illustrate how to implement a Goal ZERO approach in a constructive manner combining the power of strong leadership, people, culture, systems, and assets. The book provides a foundation on which to build a culture of mutual trust in your organization and unleash the creativity and innovation of your people.

# CHAPTER 2

## A Drive for Excellence

One of my favorite quotes from Vince Lombardi, the famous professional football coach, is "Gentlemen, we are going to relentlessly chase perfection, knowing full well we will not catch it, because nothing is perfect. But we are going to relentlessly chase it because in the process we will catch excellence. I am not remotely interested in just being good."

I always feel the same way and hope that you do too. Excellence is defined as "the quality of being outstanding or extremely good." Synonyms for excellent and excellence are distinction, first rate, superb, blue chip, choice, first class, five-star, top notch, top shelf, and numero uno.

People want their company to be excellent, but most companies are good at best. You have to work just as hard to be good as to be excellent. If you have a mediocre organization and have frequent incidents, defects, and problems; you work even harder dealing with the problems and constantly playing catchup.

In business, there are many obvious reasons why a drive for excellence is important. One good reason is offensive: excellence positions your organization in a superior manner relative to the others. Your products and services are best in class and consistently exceed your customer expectations, resulting in added value creating opportunities.

Another good reason is a defensive one: excellence in your product, services, or operations helps to preserve value in the organization by preventing major problems and defects from occurring. In the book, I'll give several examples of how companies have experienced fatal incidents with workers, significant reputation loss, and billions of dollars in property damage and business interruption from subpar operations. A drive for excellence at all times is the only way to succeed and win.

# Priorities are Constantly Changing

Following World War II, industrial capacity across the world was devastated and lacking. Since the battles had not been fought on its mainland, the United States was in an envious position to supply the world's needs. This specific period ushered in global expansion for many American companies from the 1950s to the 1970s. The main priority at that time was producing products and getting them to the customers. The customers desperately needed the products.

Quality and cost were secondary considerations. I remember older Dow colleagues telling me about product quality during those years. The specification would call for a clear liquid and periodically the delivered product might be amber. The customer would complain, and the salesman would ask, "Do you want the product or not?" The customer begrudgingly took it since there was no other choice.

By the 1970s and 1980s, Germany, Japan, and a few other countries had rebuilt production capacity and became leaders in product quality. W. Edwards Deming had been sent by the United States to Japan following World War II, where he successfully taught statistical methods for improving quality and consistency. The Deming Prize is awarded annually in Japan for individuals and companies for their contributions to the field of Total Quality Management (TQM). W. Edwards Deming's book, Out of the Crisis, is a classic and a must read.

Companies in the United States began to fall behind because of inferior quality in a wide variety of industries such as automotive and electronics. No longer did a company just need to produce a product, now consistent and superior quality was expected and demanded. Deming returned to the United States and the quality movement took center stage in the United States and around the world. Quality experts such as Joseph Juran, Philip Crosby and others were in high demand. Conventional wisdom at the time said the customer would pay a premium price for quality but that sentiment only lasted a short time. Premium quality simply opened the door for the sale.

In the early 1990s, several notable changes occurred that reshaped the industry landscape again. Global trade agreements further opened global markets. The internet began to emerge, improving global communication. Foreign companies accelerated their presence in the United States. Companies began to produce and ship products as global companies rather than country by country.

One example was Formosa Plastics, a Taiwanese company, who built a chemical plant in Point Comfort, Texas, and provided low-cost competition we had not seen previously. Dow and most other American companies had high-cost structures, conducted considerable research and development, provided excellent employee benefits, and donated heavily to the communities in which they served. Formosa, on the other hand, came to the United States with a lean cost structure with almost no additional costs other than to make and ship the product. Companies like Formosa changed the competitive landscape.

Thus, the urgent focus on cost control began in the early 1990s. Companies had to tighten spending in order to compete. The same occurred in Europe and across the world. No longer was competition with other companies in the same country, competition was on a global scale. Shipping products around the world became easier, so a high-cost producer didn't survive very long.

Today's continuous advancements in information technology and artificial intelligence enhance our ability to communicate, transfer information, monitor, and control operations better than ever before. The tools and capability for enhanced quality control are constantly improving.

The point of this brief "history of the world" story is that the competitive environment is constantly changing. We have migrated from a focus on production, to a focus on production and quality, and finally to a focus on production and quality and cost. All three elements are critical in today's world to compete and excel. Operational Excellence is a differentiator with any organization. New technology development, of course, has always been a major factor in leapfrogging the competition.

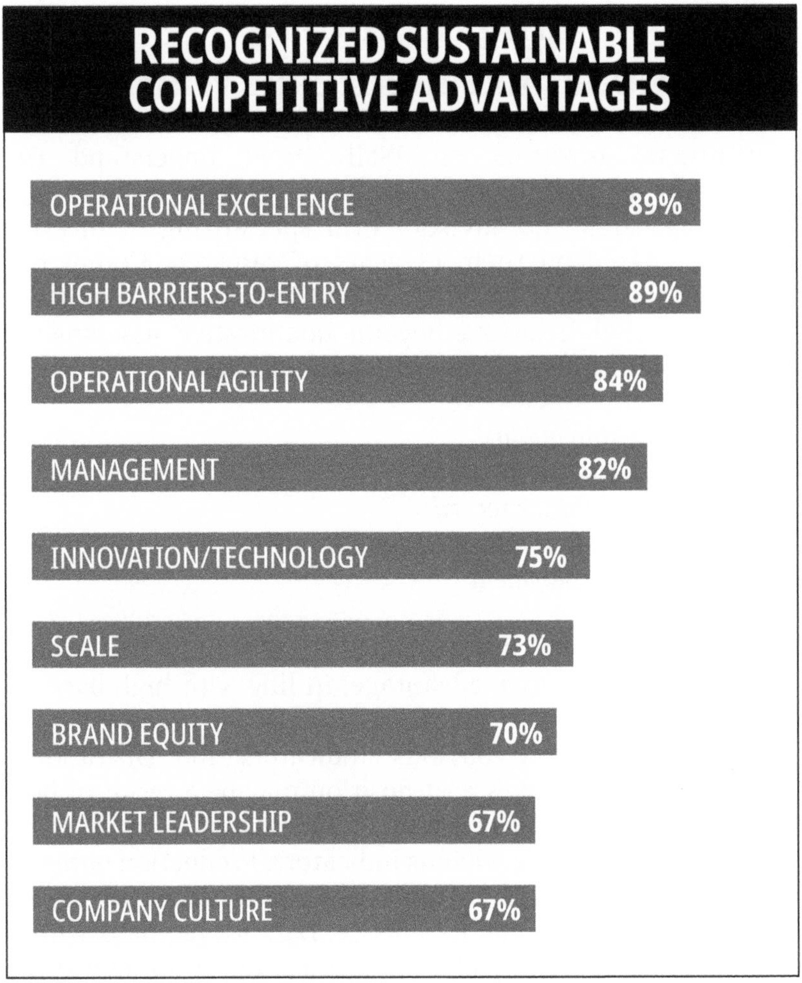

## RECOGNIZED SUSTAINABLE COMPETITIVE ADVANTAGES

| | |
|---|---|
| OPERATIONAL EXCELLENCE | 89% |
| HIGH BARRIERS-TO-ENTRY | 89% |
| OPERATIONAL AGILITY | 84% |
| MANAGEMENT | 82% |
| INNOVATION/TECHNOLOGY | 75% |
| SCALE | 73% |
| BRAND EQUITY | 70% |
| MARKET LEADERSHIP | 67% |
| COMPANY CULTURE | 67% |

**FIGURE 3**
**Priorities of Institutional Investors for Sustainable Competitive**
**Advantages Corbin Proprietary Research: Inside the Buy-side**
**Source: Corbin Advisors, 2020**

# Importance of Operational Excellence on Wall Street

Institutional investors on Wall Street understand the importance of Operational Excellence. Corbin Advisors is a leading research and advisory firm specializing in investor relations. Based on their 13 years of research, Corbin has identified the Critical Five investment factors most important to institutional investors beyond quantitative assessments when evaluating an investment. These include:

*1 Leadership quality*
*2 Sound long-term strategy*
*3 Execution track record*
*4 Sustainable competitive advantages*
*5 Capital deployment*

Investors identified Operational Excellence as the leading sustainable competitive advantage, in line with high barriers to entry (Figure 3).

There are many obvious indicators for Operational Excellence. A company's cost position may be a result of how efficient the company operates. Reliability of operation and quality of products are obvious indicators. Production outages, force majeure events, and significant quality incidents are all indicators of Operational Excellence. Data for regulatory fines and penalties for safety and environmental performance are in the public domain. The number and frequency of defects are important, but the consequences of a major event can be enormous. I'll provide several examples of major incidents to illustrate the point.

# The Consequences of a Major Incident

Unfortunately, far too many terrible incidents and crisis situations have occurred throughout history. They can happen in any industry and to any company. And more disturbing, they needlessly continue to occur, resulting in lives lost, billions of dollars in cost, business loss, and declining lack of trust in companies, industries, and government. This chart(Figure 4) reflects the recent trend of insurance losses due to significant incidents.

The trend of increasing insurance claims across a period of 10 years is alarming. Much worse is when someone dies or gets critically injured. Such an event is a tragedy and is completely

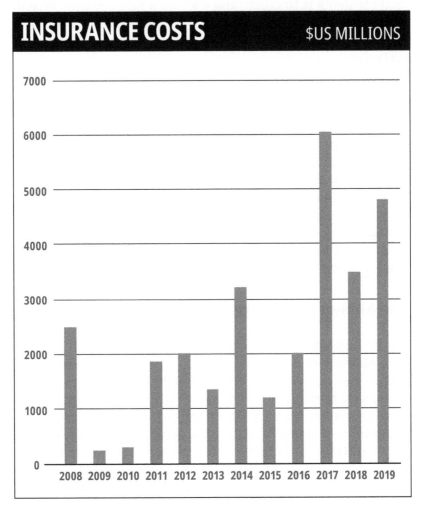

**FIGURE 4**
**Property Damage and Business Interruption**
**Source: Liberty Specialty Markets**

unacceptable. Every incident can be prevented. Every person has family members, co-workers, and friends. A personal incident impacts the entire community around the injured or deceased person and is never forgotten.

Why do these incidents keep occurring? Generally, the incidents can be traced to a breakdown in the execution of the management system (if the company even has one). The root causes may be a combination of leadership, people, culture, system, or asset failures. One of the foundations for preventing such incidents is to create and execute a management system in a proactive manner that captures learnings from the past and achieves Operational Excellence with a Goal ZERO mindset every day.

The following sections provide several examples of things going badly wrong. Unfortunately, I could have given you a hundred examples. I'm always confounded by companies that gain an increased sense of urgency for Operational Excellence *after* a crisis or major incident. Why do they wait? Terrible incidents can happen to even the best companies, but you significantly reduce the odds with a proactive, disciplined focus on Operational Excellence. These events, sadly, were all preventable and didn't have to occur. If reading these summaries doesn't give you an increased sense of urgency about being proactive, I don't know what will. Don't ever let "the big event" happen in your company.

## The Memory of Andre and Nicole

The first incident is one that I will never forget, which I named "The Memory of Andre and Nicole." This incident occurred at a retail station in Central America in 2006. One of the station employees attempted to change out a filter on one of the gasoline pumps. He hadn't been trained well on the procedure and gasoline began to spill from the pump. The gasoline ignited and engulfed a car in flames. Eleven-year-old Andre and nine-year-old Nicole were trapped inside of the car and perished in the terrible incident. As in all service stations, this station had an emergency cutoff switch on the front of the station, but people were slow to activate it.

This tragic event is one that I have used many times through the years to illustrate the importance of even the smallest of details in preventing major incidents. Companies must have good operating procedures, employees must have the skills and competence to do the job, people must know the risks involved in their work, they need to focus from start to finish, and they need to be prepared for emergency response. As in all cases, this tragic incident was preventable.

Remember, tragic incidents impact lives. In the following examples, think about the many real people such as Andre and Nicole that have been impacted.

## The Great Texas Freeze of 2021

In February 2021, the state of Texas experienced a deep freeze that doesn't occur very often. Officials of manufacturing and utility plants had a false sense of security that they were protected against the freezing weather, but many of them turned out to be wrong. Many power plants, water supplies, gas processing industries, refineries, and chemical plants shut down operations due to the freeze. Millions of people suffered for days without power and water, and there were many deaths associated with the loss of electricity.

There was significant finger pointing for who was to blame and what the causes were. But one root cause, for certain, was that many of the facilities were not as protected for the freeze as management had thought they were or expected them to be. For example, the requirements and procedures for installing heat tracing and insulation for instrumentation for hard, extended freezes are much different than for a light freeze.

Although not a common occurrence in Texas, there had been similar hard freezing conditions in 1983 and 1989. The companies should investigate these incidents, implement corrective actions, document the learnings in their management system, properly train people, and maintain assets in the right condition to be properly prepared in the future. The economic loss, human misery, and loss of life for this 2021 Texas freeze were significant.

## Blue Bell Ice Cream

Blue Bell Creameries, a 111-year-old company, headquartered in Brenham, Texas, is one of the most popular ice cream brands (my favorite) across Texas and beyond. In 2015, a crisis for the company occurred when listeria was discovered in some of its products, resulting in illnesses and three deaths. The result was product recalls and the eventual shutdown of the company's facilities. Blue Bell suffered incredible reputation damage. Federal investigators stated that Blue Bell had found evidence of listeria as early as 2013 but had failed to implement corrective actions sufficient to prevent a recurrence from happening.

The company pleaded guilty to two misdemeanor charges and paid nearly $20 million in settlements. It was involved in voluminous litigation and various settlements. The CEO was charged with seven felonies. The Board of Directors was criticized for not having a board-level food safety committee and not providing appropriate risk management oversight. Corrective actions included equipment redesign and improvements in employee and hygiene practices.

## Boeing

In March 2019, the Boeing 737 MAX passenger airliner was grounded worldwide after 346 people died in two crashes: Lion Air Flight 601 on October 29, 2018, and Ethiopian Airlines Flight 302 on March 10, 2019. The plane's stabilizing software, known as the Maneuvering Characteristics Augmentation System (the MCAS) is widely considered to be the principal cause of both crashes. Investigations revealed technical design flaws, insufficient pilot training, leadership failures, and a lack of transparency with regulators and customers.

How could this system failure happen to such a great company? The crisis was a serious blow to Boeing's reputation. The confidence of customers and the flying public was shaken, which will take years to recover. The result was the grounding of the entire 737 MAX global fleet. Boeing issued statements regarding the various corrective actions it took including strengthening the safety culture in the company, improved aircraft software and pilot training, and created a Safety Committee for the Board of Directors.

## BP Texas City

On March 23, 2005, a hydrocarbon vapor cloud ignited and violently exploded at the BP Texas City Refinery. The explosion killed 15 workers, injured 180 others and severely damaged the refinery. The hydrocarbon release resulted from liquid overflow from a blowdown stack. This chemical release followed overfilling and overheating of a process tower during startup operations. The majority of the fatalities occurred from people working in a portable building in an area adjacent to the operating unit.

Numerous investigations by a variety of entities (BP internal investigation, the Chemical Safety Board investigation, and the BP independent investigation by the Baker Panel) concluded the causes of the incident, injuries, and fatalities were numerous and represented a breakdown in BP's management system. Deficiencies included lack of addressing previously identified risks, insufficient training, lack of competent people on plant startup, lack of infrastructure investments, use of ineffective procedures that were often not followed, inoperative alarms, and siting of portable buildings too close to the unit. These are all management system items that are thoroughly covered throughout this book. Suffice to say, this incident was devastating for the families, BP, and the industry.

## BP Deepwater Horizon Oil Spill

BP experienced a second disaster five years later on April 20, 2010, at the Deepwater Horizon drilling rig in the Gulf of Mexico. Methane gas expanded in the marine riser and rose into the drilling rig where it ignited and exploded, engulfing the platform in flames. Eleven workers died in the explosion and 94 others were rescued by lifeboat or helicopter. The resulting oil spill continued until it was finally capped on September 19, 2010. The environmental damage was widespread, and the event dominated the U.S. and world news for many months. The incident is widely considered the largest marine oil spill in the history of the petroleum industry.

The investigations that followed determined deficiencies such as schedule and cost pressures, operating practices, insufficient integrity assurance, leadership and employee actions, and fear of reporting safety issues by personnel. BP was accused of lacking an adequate company safety culture.

## Pacific Gas & Electric (PG&E) Fires of 2017 and 2018

Fires sparked by equipment owned by the California utility company, PG&E, killed more than 100 people and destroyed more than 15,000 homes in northern California in 2017 and 2018. One of the fires, the 2018 Camp Fire, which devastated the city of Paradise (population 26,000), was started when a worn piece of metal known as a C-hook broke free from a transmission tower, dropping a high-voltage power line that sent molten embers onto the dry brush below.

In addition to filing bankruptcy and incurring huge liability claims, PG&E pleaded guilty to 84 counts of manslaughter for the 2018 Camp Fire, making it one of the few U.S. corporations to be convicted of homicide-related charges. Investigations revealed the company had known for years that some of its transmission lines posed serious risks but did little to address the risks. PG&E was accused of insufficient inspections, poor maintenance, and employing inspectors with improper training.

# Preventing the Big Event

The sense of urgency for action in these companies immediately after the big events was incredibly high, as you can imagine. When a company experiences such a tragedy, it expends an enormous amount of effort in corrective actions to prevent such an event from ever occurring again. But why do companies wait until after such an event to develop a sense of urgency for Operational Excellence?

Big events such as explosions, reactive chemical incidents, food contamination in the food industry, and major quality incidents are life-threatening and devastating to any business. You must make every effort possible and never lose focus on preventing tragedies from ever occurring in your company.

Maintaining a vibrant risk management program is critical. Risk management is widely known in the industry; but when it gets too complicated and diluted, it becomes ineffective. The preferred philosophy is to prioritize and clearly identify the highest potential risks, assign clear owners for each risk, and then make sure that special precautions are in place, well understood, and executed to perfection at all times.

Companies regularly train and remind employees (and especially leaders) of these top risks and the potential consequences if the big event were to occur. This training should include a summary of the proactive measures that must be maintained to perfection at all times.

Over the years, there have been too many major incidents from lost knowledge and experience due to people moving on to other jobs or retiring. Terrible incidents continue to occur because people forget or become lax in maintaining any and all preventative measures. As time goes by, people tend to focus on other areas and forget the learnings of the past.

This loss of institutional knowledge should never occur! For the most critical risks, you can't afford to rely on people's memories; exactly the reason why a robust management system is so important at loss prevention, protecting people, and protecting the wealth of a firm. A management system provides a constant, systemic focus on proactive measures to assure operations are conducted the right way, every time.

*GOAL ZERO NUGGET:*
*Create a sense of urgency in your organization.*

# The Small Things Count

Have you heard the shoe tying story from the great college basketball coach, John Wooden? Wooden was the coach of the University of California (UCLA) basketball team from 1948 to 1975. His team dominated and won 10 national championships over 12 consecutive years.

At the first practice of each season, John Wooden would say, "Men, this is how you put your shoes and socks on." He would commence to show them the basic techniques of shoe tying. Some of the returning players had been through this before; however, it didn't matter, they were going to review it again. Learning to tie shoes properly was vital to Wooden. It meant star players would never get a blister that would keep them from playing. A team can't be its best unless everyone's able to play.

I'm a firm believer that great results come from doing the little things right all of the time. Thousands of examples illustrate how relatively small items have resulted in catastrophic results:

- *A faulty O-Ring in the 1986 Space Shuttle Challenger explosion*
- *A minor design change by a valve manufacturer causing a significant explosion*
- *An insufficient integrity check on a major capital project*
- *Wrong material of construction slipping into use*
- *Single instrument giving a false indication*
- *Individual turning a wrong valve*

Undoubtedly, one of the best ways to prevent incidents is to make sure everyone pays attention to detail at all times, task by task. I have participated in far more investigations than I care to remember where the root cause of a major incident was typically the result of not following the process or inattention to detail. All of these incidents were preventable. That's why long ago, I realized *The Power of Goal ZERO* on even the smallest of items in each of the categories I have mentioned earlier: leadership, people, culture, systems, and assets.

The point of this section is that all of the small things matter if you truly want your company to excel. Goal ZERO helps to make the concept clear for people. Establish a Goal ZERO culture and mindset for everything, and you will stand a much better chance of avoiding not only small incidents but also significantly large ones.

**GOAL ZERO NUGGET:**
*Pay attention to small details.*

# Moving Forward
# with Operational Excellence

Let's turn now to the concept of Operational Excellence. It's important to look at the big picture and understand how everything fits together in developing a world-class, winning organization. You must understand the model clearly and be able to explain it to others. Albert Einstein said, "If you can't explain it simply, then you don't understand it well enough." I personally feel that a concept should be as intuitive as possible to help people fully endorse it.

Profitability, customer satisfaction, Operational Excellence, safety, and winning are all lagging indicators of how well an organization performs. Many organizations set long term goals for these objectives without specific plans of how to achieve them. Some leaders are very articulate and talk a good game, but don't deliver the results. I call these leaders the "articulate incompetent." Milton Friedman once said, "One of the great mistakes is to judge policies and programs by their intentions rather than their results." You can't wish your way to good performance, profitability, and winning. To achieve your desired results (lagging indicators), it's vital to deliver measurable results on the drivers that will most impact your ultimate objectives.

Operational Excellence is a lagging indicator for organizational performance, but it's a critical intermediate step for accomplishing your ultimate objectives of reliability, customer satisfaction, and profitability. Let's begin with my formula for Operational Excellence and some short definitions to illustrate the drivers that it takes. I'll build on each of these components as the book progresses.

# Operational Excellence =
# Leadership + People + Culture + Systems + Assets

- **Operational Excellence.** *A desired state in which everything goes right most of the time. In two organizations with the same strategy, the one that achieves better Operational Excellence will generally have superior reliability, safety, quality, consistency, cost control, profitably, governance, and value creation.*
- **Leadership.** *The art of successfully leading a group of individuals towards achieving a common goal.*
- **People.** *Talented, competent, motivated individuals that work together to achieve a common goal.*
- **Culture.** *The beliefs, behavior, attitude, outlook, values, morals, and customs of an organization. Many factors contribute to the culture of an organization.* **Goal ZERO** *is a leadership tool that provides people with a different way of thinking and enhances a culture of doing things the right way at all times and winning.*
- **Systems.** *A documented collection of knowledge, technology, best practices, processes, procedures, and consistent ways of doing work. For larger organizations, a system will exist at the corporate level and associated systems will be in place at the local level for more detailed procedures and other pertinent documents. A system is commonly referred to as a* **Management System.**
- **Assets.** *The facilities, equipment, and tools that an organization uses and operates to accomplish its work. Well designed and maintained assets are essential, especially in a manufacturing company.*

Many companies are very good at one or more of the categories listed above. However, the truly superior companies master them all. If you are mediocre in any of the listed categories, you will never achieve world-class Operational Excellence on a consistent basis. It's about the power of *AND:* leadership, people, culture, systems, *AND* assets. These five items must be approached in an integrated manner for maximum performance achievement.

I have often been asked, "What is most important—safety, quality, or reliability?" Don't let anyone drag you into this discussion about choosing one or the other. A Goal ZERO culture means zero defects for everything.

If you don't manage your costs and make a profit, the company won't survive. Issues in quality and reliability will destroy customer satisfaction and customers will run to the competition. Environmental incidents are wrong ethically and will cause you to lose your license to operate. And safety— everyone knows protecting people is critical, but too many companies get serious only after a serious incident occurs. The answer is that you must address all aspects in a proactive way under a common umbrella of Operational Excellence.

No one doubts the importance of Operational Excellence. But make no mistake about it, achieving Operational Excellence is hard work. But you can make the work easier and more efficient for yourself and your organization if you break it down into these understandable categories. You are most likely already working in each of the categories listed above but may have not organized the focus in this way. A functioning management system captures best practices so that the organization can continually improve and win.

# The System Approach

One of the reasons given for incidents is people retiring and leaving the workforce. The knowledge is going out the door. Another cause frequently discussed is people forgetting learnings years after an incident occurred. These reasons focus on the loss of experience rather than the lack of a good system to capture those experiences.

Addressing loss of institutional knowledge is one of the primary reasons I have written this book and specifically this section about Operational Excellence Management Systems. A well-functioning management system will prevent this loss of knowledge. Most leaders will say they have a management system, but I wonder if their systems are fully utilized and effective. Many systems don't have good processes for continually capturing knowledge and information. A good management system documents all learnings from the past in an understandable manner, so the learnings are constantly integrated into daily work and are never forgotten. People can leave but the knowledge remains. You should never repeat the same incident twice, no matter how much time has gone by.

There are so many analogies between business and sports. Both have competitors. Both are committed to winning. Both take discipline, talented people, a game plan, and flawless execution. Let's take football, for example.

One of my favorite football coaches is Nick Saban at the University of Alabama. In 2021, he notched his seventh National Championship in college football. Saban is considered one of the greatest college football coaches of all time. Saban is one coach that gets it. If you listen to him speak, he always talks about "the system." He figured out and understood the power of a management system years ago. He has continually updated and perfected his system on a regular basis. He'll tell you that when he hires a new assistant coach, he wants the coach to come in and learn the Alabama system; not operate by his previous practices. Saban knows that if every new coach comes in and does things his own way, the team will never have consistency or establish excellence.

This doesn't mean the knowledge and processes the new coach brings are not valued. I'm sure that Nick Saban listens to ideas from new coaches and updates his "system" as appropriate to capture new and better concepts.

Saban's "system" includes processes for every aspect of his operation: how the organization identifies and accesses talent, how they recruit, how they onboard their new players and coaches (including how to tie your shoes), how they conduct practices, how they prepare for games, how they prepare their players mentally, how they conduct the game, how they call the plays, how they make sure every player executes every play flawlessly, how they analyze the game afterward, and how they make corrections as needed. Guess what? His team wins on a consistent basis.

If you watch Nick Saban on the sideline, it doesn't matter if his team is 30 points ahead (normally) or 30 points behind (almost never), he goes crazy if a player makes an unnecessary mistake. He's continually focused on flawless execution on every play no matter the score. He understands that in football, the only thing each player can do is to perform flawlessly on each play, one play at a time. If every player executes to perfection on every play throughout the game, the team has a good chance of winning. Due to his focus and understanding of the importance of a system, it's obvious why the old saying is true, "He can take his team and beat you, and take your team and beat you!"

Saban has developed his plan (the system) over the years which allows him to focus almost entirely on his players' execution. On the rare occasion that his team loses, you won't hear him say that he needs to figure out what went wrong and wonder about what needs to be done differently as you hear from so many mediocre coaches. Instead, he'll talk about going back and working on better execution of the system. Saban definitely understands the value of a good management system.

Now let's get back to "the system" for business. You often hear the saying, "The best defense is a good offense." I believe this saying directly applies to business. I would much rather run my business proactively based on a system that has been thoroughly developed through the years and keeps getting better. Spend your time focusing on the flawless execution of your management system, especially the people aspects. Too many organizations wait for problems to occur and then spend countless hours investigating and figuring out how to prevent the problems from occurring again. This is a backward and reactive approach.

In today's global environment with communication tools and social media, bad news travels fast. Your company is only as good as its weakest link. A major incident occurring in a single location in the world can have devastating consequences and potentially bring down the organization. We used to say, "When part of the skunk stinks, the entire skunk stinks." Therefore, you can no longer afford to have every location operate its facility entirely its own way as we did in the ancient past. Changing operating practices each time leadership changes has inherently higher risk, increased turmoil, and never leads to overall company consistency and Operational Excellence.

# What Do You Really Want to Achieve? Are You Serious?

I've described the concepts of Goal ZERO, Operational Excellence, and the tragic consequences that can occur from a significant incident. You must ask yourself if you are serious about taking your organization to the next level. It doesn't matter if you are the CEO or an engineer in an operating unit, what level of intensity do you have for Goal ZERO and Operational Excellence? Does everyone around you see and feel the intensity and expectations that you have?

Inherently, everyone agrees and fundamentally understands the importance of Operational Excellence, but where does leadership spend most of its time? In my experience, most of the time spent in corporate leadership team and Board of Director meetings is on financial items—business strategy, earnings, cost management, customers, growth and mergers and acquisitions. This allocation changes, however, *after* a major incident or operational problem occurs. The focus then changes to a reactive mode, but it's too late; the damage has already been done.

Plenty of people monitor the financial results of a company. Wall Street has a laser focus on quarterly earnings. Countless investor calls and meetings take place throughout the year. The Board of Directors constantly focuses on earnings and the strategy going forward. This emphasis trickles down through the CEO, the leadership team, and the entire organization. And finally, each department is held accountable for cost management and earnings growth for the business units. Financial metrics are very clear and easy to track.

This financial focus is all perfectly understandable and, of course, very important. The smartest leaders, however, understand that financial results are *lagging indicators* of actions and performance. The key is a focus on the drivers of performance in a passionate and obvious manner. Every company has strategies and plans but many companies fail in the execution of those plans. A manufacturing company will never achieve excellence in profitability if there is mediocre performance in operations, reliability, quality, and safety.

How much time is spent in your organization in a proactive way on Operational Excellence? Are you serious about Operational Excellence and do you demand and expect excellence at all times? Tone at the top and constancy of purpose lead the way in establishing a Goal ZERO culture across the company.

An old Chinese proverb is pertinent when evaluating your approach to Goal ZERO performance and Operational Excellence: "If you want to know your past, look into your present conditions. If you want to know your future, look into your present actions."

**GOAL ZERO NUGGET:**
*Every company has strategies and plans but
many companies fail to execute.*

# Bad, Good, or Great

We are all customers in our personal lives and business. At the highest level, we all want the same things: a good quality product, consistency, availability when I need it and at a reasonable price. We also know how frustrating it can be when we pay good money and don't receive the expected product or service.

I've often told the story about how a restaurant can reside in one of three categories: **bad, good,** or **great.** We can all relate to this model whether it's a restaurant or any other type of establishment.

If you dine at a restaurant and the food or service is **bad,** you probably won't go back. The damage is already done. Even worse, you'll tell our friends about the experience. The result is a rippling effect for the reputation of the establishment; and customers never forget.

The second category, and most common, is that the food or service was **good,** but not anything special. People don't normally talk about these kinds of establishments to others because so many restaurants fall into this category. You may return, or you might go somewhere else the next time. It really doesn't matter because you have other choices.

The final category is the **great** restaurant. The food is outstanding and consistent every time. The service is impeccable. The restaurant is clean and has an inviting atmosphere. You and your family or friends eagerly look forward to every visit. The food and drink prices may be higher, but the place is so popular that you have to make reservations way ahead of time. You brag about this kind of restaurant to others. People line up for a chance to dine there. The great reputation travels far and wide. This kind of establishment differentiates itself from the competition, and the results are enormous.

We always drove hard for our businesses to be in the great category. Even a commodity business can differentiate itself from the competition by a constant focus on product consistency, on-time delivery and mistake free performance. Satisfied customers of good companies are not good enough, because they might switch. Strive to have loyal customers who won't go anywhere else.

When your customers brag about your products and service, you are on your way to becoming great. And it's relatively easy to differentiate your company because most of the competitors are good at best. In other words, achieve greatness through a systematic approach of Operational Excellence and a consistent Goal ZERO mindset. Insist on zero defects at all times. Treat every incident as a big deal, learn from it, and keep driving for perfection. Good isn't good enough anymore. Be great.

# Setting Expectations

Everyone is familiar with Missions and Visions. Many "statements" are long sentences that capture everything under the sun. While these documents are good at a high level, they don't do much to actually change behavior and drive improvement.

The purpose of Mission and Vision documents is to state the values and intention of the organization. In other words, they describe the organizational vision for items such as safety, quality, environment, reliability, cost, profitability, sustainability, and ethics.

A good Code of Conduct is also essential for any organization. It establishes the moral compass for the company and individuals and should include topics such as ethical behavior, legal requirements, conflict of interest, protecting intellectual property, dealing fairly with others, human rights, and record keeping.

In addition to the Mission, Vision, and Code of Conduct documents, I highly recommend an **Operational Excellence Expectations Document** for your organization. This document is simple to read, is understandable, and establishes very clear **expectations** for every individual and department in the company that will lead to a Goal ZERO culture. Leadership teams can work together to develop the Expectations Document for your workforce. The exercise is extremely useful in creating alignment and commitment. Each expectation is written in a clear and positive manner.

The best way to organize the expectations is to list them under each area of importance such as leadership, people, operations, risk management, assessment, and improvement. The number of expectations is a matter of choice. As an example, ExxonMobil has 65 expectations and LyondellBasell has 40. The primary objective is to clearly state what you expect from people across your organization. Just remember, once you write it, you then need to walk the talk! I've included examples of items you might include in your Operational Excellence Expectations Document.

## Operational Excellence Expectations—Examples

1. *Individual Accountability. Leaders, employees, and contractors are responsible for meeting applicable company rules and requirements, working safely, avoiding mistakes, identifying hazards, preventing unsafe work practices, and reporting unsafe conditions.*
2. *Competency. Employees and contractors have the necessary skills and knowledge to perform their jobs.*
3. *Ethics and Integrity. Leaders insist on compliance with laws, regulations, and internal requirements, effectively monitor performance, and take action to correct all deficiencies.*

4. ***Management System.*** *Leaders assure that their management system is kept up-to-date and that the expectations of the company are being met.*

5. ***Reporting.*** *Employees and contractors report potential violations of legal or company policy without fear of retribution.*

6. ***Learning from Experience.*** *Management systems are updated to capture internal and external learning.*

7. ***Risk Management Process.*** *Hazards are systematically identified, owners are assigned, risk assessments are conducted, and mitigation measures are put in place.*

8. ***Technology.*** *Technology is continually advanced and documented in the management system.*

9. ***Procedures.*** *Operating, maintenance, and inspection procedures are in place, kept up to date, and are rigorously followed.*

10. ***Management of Change.*** *A management of change process is rigorously followed for people, process, and equipment changes.*

11. ***Incident Reporting and Investigation.*** *Incidents and high-potential near misses are promptly reported, investigated, and priority action items are defined.*

12. ***Communications and dialogue.*** *Key stakeholders are identified, and good relations are maintained through communication and dialogue.*

13. ***Self-Assessment.*** *Regular, ongoing self-assessments with timely corrective actions take place to ensure adherence to legal and internal requirements.*

14. ***Audits.*** *Independent, comprehensive audits with timely corrective actions take place to ensure adherence to legal and internal requirements.*

16. ***Action Item Closure.*** *Action items from self-assessments, audits, investigations, and risk reviews are completed by their assigned due dates.*

17. ***Management System Review.*** *An annual self-assessment of the management system takes place to evaluate its suitability, adequacy, and effectiveness.*

Print the Expectations Document in a pamphlet and distribute to all of your employees and contractors. The

Expectations Document provides an excellent platform for employee discussions around the world. Discuss your vision for achieving Operational Excellence in all that you do. You need a Goal ZERO approach to each of the Expectations listed in the document. By constant messaging and with all leadership totally aligned, you will experience a rapid shift in employee mindset and level of compliance. Good communication helps your workforce to understand the objectives you are trying to achieve as a company and why they were important.

I believe the most important expectation is the first one on Individual Accountability, which states the expectation for each employee to *work safely and follow all rules*. This expectation may seem obvious but be sure to repeat this individual expectation over and over to embed it in people's minds. Individual accountability at all levels is critical to achieving Goal ZERO performance.

The second one simply states that employees and contractors must have the skills and competencies to do the job. Don't perform any task unless you are prepared. No employee can give the excuse that he/she wasn't trained; make the expectation clear that no person should even attempt a job or task if he/she doesn't believe he/she is qualified.

It's relatively easy to write a document and then put it on the shelf. However, make sure everyone is committed to achieving the expectations you have established. To close the loop, survey each employee as to adherence to each expectation every time a particular site or department receives an Operational Excellence audit. Separate the responses from supervisors and employees of the audited department. As you can imagine, if the answers between the two groups are different, the difference gives you something to discuss further.

Be serious about a Goal ZERO approach to the Operational Excellence Expectations and don't accept lip service as to compliance. You will never receive any pushback on the expectations if they are written in a commonsense manner and your people understand the importance.

**GOAL ZERO NUGGET:**
*Great leaders make expectations extremely clear.*

# Leadership Alignment

Each of my three multinational companies was unique in its own way and had different starting points regarding Operational Excellence. In all cases, we made great progress with significant improvement in results. The consistent approach was in creating a compelling vision and driving change to achieve the vision. However, I always wanted to go faster with a higher sense of urgency. I'll describe some methods I believe will increase your efficiency and drive rapid transformation in your organization.

Successful change management requires considerable discussion, communication, and flexibility to bring the entire organization along. In the end, you want your people to truly believe in the path forward and feel they have all been part of its development. It's a wonderful feeling when your team is aligned on a common mission and everyone works enthusiastically towards the same goal.

One of the most important factors in making major change in an organization is to assure there is *understanding, alignment, and support of top leadership.* To be most effective, Operational Excellence needs to be company-wide and cut across traditional functional boundaries in organizations. Breaking down functional barriers is an important concept and difficult to achieve in many companies that have strong functions. Turf battles are common. It's critical that leadership at the top understands and insists on a company-wide approach with each function working closely together and in alignment.

Another common challenge in large companies is an independent focus on improvement within each individual function rather than companywide. Functions such as Manufacturing, Quality, Personal Safety, Process Safety, Environment, Reliability, and Human Resources often have independent strategies and plans for improvement. They are all working hard but not necessarily in a smart and coordinated manner. This independent approach often includes different terminology and concepts which add complexity and confuses the organization.

A better approach is to keep the focus at a higher level under the umbrella of Operational Excellence. Operational Excellence provides an overall corporate approach from the top of the organization, which improves clarity and consistency. An Operational Excellence approach allows each function and location to work within an overall framework to provide proper attention for its specific areas of responsibility. Operational Excellence also eliminates the discussion about which is most important: safety, reliability, quality, cost, etc. The answer is that Operational Excellence is most important and all of these items are included

We broke down functional barriers at LyondellBasell by the creation of an Operational Excellence Leadership Team (OELT). The mission for the team was clear, to provide a coordinated approach to achieving Operational Excellence in the organization. I managed the team and membership included the Executive Vice President of Manufacturing, the General Counsel, the Chief Human Resources Officer and a Vice President of a business unit. Remember that with a Goal ZERO mentality, compliance is mandatory, and requirements typically have people, legal, and cost implications.

You don't typically find legal and human resources people on such high-level Operational Excellence teams, but I can't emphasize the importance of their participation enough. Operational Excellence is not just an Operational or EH&S responsibility, it takes all of the major functions working together. Breaking down and eliminating functional silos and barriers is critical. Each function must be completely on board and aligned with the mission if you want Operational Excellence in the company to be successful.

I encourage you to establish your own version of a multifunctional OELT if you embark on a major improvement initiative of your Operational Excellence system. The primary objectives of the OELT are to assure alignment on strategy and approach, resolve issues, provide governance over the system, approve new standards or requirements, assure each function is contributing to success, and assess the progress.

**GOAL ZERO NUGGET:**
*Effective change management
requires strong leadership alignment.*

# Results Focused

This section is included to simply demonstrate that the concepts presented in this book actually work and deliver rapid results. The results achieved in our companies not only saved lives and protected people but also contributed to operations becoming more reliable and improving quality thus resulting in better customer satisfaction and countless other benefits.

We always worked together as a team with a common mission and vision of achieving excellence. I've always loved the saying, "It's amazing how much you can accomplish if you don't care who gets the credit." I am extremely proud of the people I worked with around the world and the results that we all achieved together. My eternal gratitude goes out to each of them.

Here are a few highlights of the results we achieved at each company. These are only EH&S statistics and don't include the additional value generated by achieving Operational Excellence. These are statistics, but every percentage of improvement represents people that did not get injured, process safety incidents that didn't occur and environmental impacts that never happened.

### Dow Chemical 2000-2004
*$32 billion in sales, 46,000 employees*
- *53% reduction in injury/illness rate*
- *41% reduction of environmental spills and releases*
- *$22 million reduction in corporate EH&S cost*

### Royal Dutch Shell 2004-2009
*$450 billion in sales, 101,000 employees*
- *47 % reduction in injury/illness rate*
- *64% reduction in lost time injury rate*
- *77% reduction in spills*

### LyondellBasell 2009-2017
*$34 billion in sales, 14,000 employees*
- *56% reduction in injury/illness rate*
- *60% reduction in environmental incidents*
- *80% reduction in process safety incidents*

# Environmental, Social and Governance (ESG)

When I became Vice President at Dow in 2000, I was asked to spend one-third of my time externally and to lead the development of the corporate strategy for Sustainable Development. I worked closely with the US EPA, OSHA, the President's Council on Environmental Quality, and various governmental regulatory agencies in the Europe and Asia. It was important to know the leaders of each organization and to build mutual trust.

I spent considerable time in dialogue with individuals at non-governmental organizations (NGOs) such as the World Resources Institute, Environmental Defense, Sierra Club, Resources for the Future, Friends of the Earth and Greenpeace. Although we rarely agreed on philosophy, I always enjoyed the interaction and gained a better understanding of their viewpoints on various issues.

As the leader for Sustainable Development and ESG in my companies, I became very involved externally to become an active part of the discussions. As time progressed, I was appointed to the Board of Directors of the World Environment Center and the International Leadership Council for the Nature Conservancy. I led the Dow delegation to the World Summit on Sustainable Development in Johannesburg, South Africa.

I enjoyed my interactions with many fascinating global opinion leaders on the subject such as John Elkington, founder of SustainAbility, Bjorn Stigson, President of the World Business Council on Sustainable Development, Tom Burke, author of *Ethics, Environment and the Company,* Julia Marton-Lefevre, Director General of the International Union for Conservation of Nature (IUCN), Maurice Strong, Executive Director of the United Nations Environment Programme, and Jonathan Lash, President of the World Resources Institute..... just to name a few.

On one occasion, I invited the Washington, D.C. government relations director of Greenpeace, to speak to our Dow Public Policy leadership team. He thought I was crazy about talking at a Dow meeting, but he eventually agreed. As I was introducing him at the meeting, he pulled a quick surprise by handcuffing himself to me. Then he said, "We are often handcuffed to fences or in the back of police cars. Now I feel comfortable." Everyone got a good laugh out of it and it helped put everyone at ease. I always enjoyed interactions with these folks and getting different perspectives on issues.

There has been much discussion and evolution through the years regarding the purpose of corporations. Milton Friedman, the 1976 Nobel Prize winner for Economic Sciences, presented the idea that the sole role of a firm is to make money for its shareholders. Concepts were changing in the late 1980s, when "Responsible Care®" became the chemical industry initiative to continually improve environment, health, safety, and security performance. A term commonly used in industry was Corporate Social Responsibility which was a form of corporate self-regulation. As time progressed, John Elkington, in 1998, published *Cannibals with Forks: The Triple Bottom Line of 21st Century Business*. In the book, he emphasized Environment, Social, and Economic issues and coined the phrase "triple bottom line." I was beginning to get involved in this space at the time and thought that it was a brilliant approach since he brought the three major special interest groups (environmental, social, and business) together for discussions and to work on the world's leading issues.

Sustainable Development was the terminology most often used at the time. In 2005, Environment, Social, and Governance (ESG) became the term commonly used for investing purposes. I believe changing Elkington's "Economic" component to a much broader "Governance" focus was another brilliant move. Governance is much more of an encompassing term, thereby attracting increased attention of investors. ESG has led to more consistent reporting of performance and is used by the capital markets as a tool for responsible investing.

After all of these years, many people still ask the same question, "How do you define sustainable development and ESG? What does it mean for us as a company?" Confusion is understandable, since it seems like almost anything can fit under the broad umbrella of ESG:

- *Environment can include topics such as climate change, emissions, depletion of resources, waste management, energy intensity, and water management.*
- *Social can cover human rights, child labor, safety, diversity, equality, inclusion, public and community support, animal welfare, and how a company manages relationships with employees, suppliers, customers, and the communities where it operates.*
- **Governance** *deals with items such as a company's leadership, management systems, audits, compliance, internal controls, operational excellence, executive pay, and shareholder rights.*

Tens of thousands of non-governmental organizations (NGOs) exist around the world. These groups focus on and drive their specific topic of interest, often as if it was the only issue to be dealt with. Social media has made it much easier for global communication and focus. You'll never have to worry about lack of attention in the public on any particular issue that you choose.

Stakeholders monitor the ESG ratings of companies through various rating agencies such as MSCI ESG, Dow Jones Sustainability Index (DJSI), Sustainalytics, and many others. Environmental and social performance are easiest to measure, but governance is softer and not as measurable. This is why leadership, Operational Excellence and the principles in this book are so important for ESG risk management. Without good governance, it's difficult to get anything else right. A high sustainability rating may look good to stakeholders but that doesn't necessarily translate to performance. Pacific Gas and Electric, for example, had been rated by ESG rating agencies as best among its peers prior to its serious fires in 2017-2018 and filing bankruptcy in 2019.

During my years of involvement and leadership in the area of sustainability and ESG, I learned invaluable lessons. One of the most important factors is to become extremely educated on the ESG issues facing society. A company must determine which of the issues are real and which ones are just noise. You must define your organization's proactive strategy for how you will approach ESG and not let others define it for you. Defining your strategy puts you on the offense, meaning that you can articulate what you are and are not doing. Remember, you will never be able to please everyone.

A crucial point is to maintain a balanced approach with environment, social, *and* governance issues. Remember, drive progress on the environmental and social challenges but don't lose focus on Operational Excellence. Integrate an ESG strategy into your business strategy and everyday work, not just an add-on. Too many companies have lost focus and, in the process, many of these companies no longer exist.

Remember to monitor ESG progress in your procurement and supply chain management. Protecting human rights in the supply chain, minimizing the impact on the environment and strong governance are all critical traits of reliable suppliers.

To help in developing your ESG strategy, it's helpful to consider "Quality of Life" models. Your organization can address these for the communities in which you operate and the broader public in general. Quality of Life factors help during discussions with community leaders by keeping the discussion focused on the big picture. Some common Quality of Life factors in a community are:

- *Economic: income, jobs, taxes, etc.*
- *Housing*
- *Health*
- *Environment*
- *Education*
- *Security*
- *Civic engagement*

The bottom line is that there doesn't have to be confusion or mystery when addressing sustainability or ESG. Be proactive, remain balanced, define your strategy, set reasonable goals, deliver measurable results, and communicate often.

**GOAL ZERO NUGGET:**
*Integrate an ESG strategy into your business strategy and everyday work.*

# "The Public" Has Diverse Opinions

Responsible Care® is the global chemical industry initiative to continually improve environment, health, safety, and security performance. The initiative began in Canada in 1984 and was adopted by the U.S. chemical industry in 1988. Participation in Responsible Care® is a condition of membership in the American Chemistry Council and all companies have made CEO level commitments to uphold the program elements.

One of the principles is to openly engage with stakeholders regarding their perspectives on various issues. Chemical industry manufacturing sites across the country, and around the world, have formed Community Advisory Panels; a terrific forum for engaging the public and encouraging interaction.

At the corporate level, Dow Chemical was the industry leader in the industry by creating a Corporate Environmental Advisory Council (CEAC) in 1992. The name was later changed to the Sustainability External Advisory Council (SEAC) and is still in existence today. The purpose is to bring a diverse outside-in perspective on issues. Council members come from around the world and include influential experts and leaders from non-governmental organizations (NGOs), academia, the business community, and governments.

When I became Vice President of EH&S at Dow and began working with the CEAC, I was incredibly impressed with each of the members and the depth of experience that each of them brought to the table. These global individuals were highly respected and enjoyed dialoging with each other as much as they did with the company. Every meeting was filled with deep discussions on the important issues of the day. The ground rules were that we wanted to hear and exchange views on various topics, but the CEAC did not vote or try to bring consensus on how Dow should proceed going forward. These guidelines allowed each member to freely express his or her opinion since there were no decisions or commitments to be made.

We discussed all types of issues such as climate change, dioxin, human rights, and testing of products. I remember my first meeting in which we presented a touchy issue we were dealing with and our planned approach. When we completed the presentation, the first CEAC member to speak gave a passionate talk on how wrong we were and why she thought so. She had my full attention.

However, the next speaker took the opposite view and said we were taking exactly the right approach. He gave an equally energetic talk on the issue. Each of these CEAC members were extremely eloquent and presented his/her case passionately. I quickly found out that on practically every topic, there were diverse opinions on both sides of the issue. The value of these discussions was to dialogue, listen and learn, and then make our own decisions on which way to proceed.

These CEAC discussions were extremely helpful to me personally and to all of us in the company. One of the clear learnings was to be careful when someone says "the public" feels one way or another about a topic, or "the public" demands or won't accept something. The fact is there are a diversity of views by people that make up "the public" and you must educate yourself on the issues to make good sound decisions. Don't allow people to generalize how "the public" feels or what "the public" is thinking.

This principle also applies to communities where you operate and the employees in your company. There aren't many community issues in which all residents have the same opinion. Take time to dialogue and learn, make decisions based on good information, and be prepared to communicate, discuss, and support your decisions. Be cautious of falling into the political correctness trap on every issue that comes along. You will never be able to please everyone.

# CHAPTER 3

## Leadership—
## Excellence Begins with You

Tone at the top and walking the talk are incredibly important aspects for any leader of an organization. A good CEO establishes the expectations, works relentlessly to assure expectations are met and removes obstacles and barriers to success.

I joined LyondellBasell in 2009 when the company had been in bankruptcy for a few months. When Jim Gallogly, the new CEO, asked me to join the company, I responded, "Why would I want to join a bankrupt chemical company? The only way that I have ever approached my job is to do things the right way. I don't want anything to do with a company that has to cut corners due to lack of money and take unreasonable risks that would put people in harm's way."

Jim smiled and said he fully agreed. His leadership philosophy was that safety was his highest priority and that we would spend whatever it took (in a cost-conscious manner of course) to increase the reliability and safety of our plants. He said growth and expansion would initially take a back seat to establishing Operational Excellence (a bold statement for a CEO). Growth would come later.

I accepted the job as Global Vice President for EH&S and Operational Excellence reporting to the CEO. Jim endorsed my Goal ZERO concept and established Operational Excellence as one of the six pillars of our company strategy. He created a strong tone at the top. We created a culture of dedication, hard work, safety, focus, teamwork, and winning.

Jim Gallogly's strong support for Operational Excellence and our outstanding LyondellBasell global personnel helped our company to become one of the most reliable, safest, and most profitable companies in the industry. We emerged from bankruptcy in April 2010 and went public in October 2010 on the New York Stock Exchange at an initial stock price of around $17/share. By 2015, the stock had reached a peak price of $115/share. The private equity firm Apollo Global Management was one of the creditors that stepped forward during bankruptcy. When Apollo divested their investment, they made approximately $9 billion in profit on a $2 billion investment. In August 2014, a Forbes magazine article stated LyondellBasell had been the best private equity deal in Wall Street history.

Gallogly received external recognition for his leadership. Dr. David Michaels was the U.S. Assistant Secretary of Labor for the Occupational Safety and Health Administration (OSHA) from 2009-2017, roughly the same time I worked for LyondellBasell. Dr. Michaels oversaw the safety for literally hundreds of companies across the country and I interacted with him on many occasions. In the March 21, 2018, edition of the Harvard Business Review, he wrote an article entitled, "7 Ways to Improve Operations Without Sacrificing Workplace Safety."

In the article, Dr. Michaels complemented Jim Gallogly as being a CEO that "did it the right way," saying, "When Gallogly arrived at LyondellBasell, the firm was in bankruptcy; his job was to return the company to profitably, which he did. At his first meeting with his employees, however, he announced that he wasn't going to begin by talking about the firm's financial challenges. Instead, the new CEO wanted to focus on something far more important: his absolute commitment to safety. He subsequently included a report of the firm's safety performance in every earnings call too."

Bob Patel succeeded Jim Gallogly as CEO of LyondellBasell in early 2015 and hit the ground running. Bob continued to drive Goal ZERO and Operational Excellence in the organization. As an example, LyondellBasell acquired A. Schulman, Inc., a leading supplier of high-performance plastic compounds, composites, and powders, in 2018. At the time of the acquisition, the OSHA injury/illness rate for the A. Schulman workforce was 1.54 (about 1 injury in a year for every 65 workers), over seven times higher than the injury/illness rate at LyondellBasell. Patel demonstrated his passion for people and communicated his Goal ZERO expectations from the beginning to the A. Schulman employees joining LyondellBasell. He knew a significant culture change would take time, but he also had full confidence that the company would be successful.

To fast forward, the acquisition of A. Schulman was successful. The new employees and businesses fully integrated into LyondellBasell and the company's management system for conducting work and the Goal ZERO culture. And most importantly, the previous A. Schulman sites made rapid improvement in safety performance nearly matching the performance of the legacy LyondellBasell sites within two years of the acquisition. LyondellBasell (including the A. Schulman acquired assets) had a combined total workforce injury/illness rate of 0.20 in 2020 (that's 1 injury in a year for every 500 workers—world-class safety performance).

Bob Patel's leadership was well recognized by the public and his peers. In 2021, LyondellBasell was named to Fortune Magazine's list of the world's most admired companies for the fourth straight year. In addition, Patel was recognized in 2018 by receiving the prestigious global chemical industry ICIS Kavaler Award (Jim Gallogly received the award in 2014). The award is selected by industry peers for the senior executive making the greatest positive impact on his/her company and the chemical industry. Patel won it again the next year, 2019, the only two-time winner in the history of the award.

I was proud to work closely with both Bob Patel and Jim Gallogly. They are two examples of results focused leaders, putting safety first and driving business success through strong Operational Excellence and influence of others.

Achieving excellence in any organization requires strong leadership. I'm talking about leadership at *all levels* setting the right example and driving change. No matter your position in the organization, you can demonstrate ownership and provide leadership to steer the organization in the right direction.

Naturally, the person at the top of a company, department, and location has the position power and the best opportunity for influence. However, I've seen culture driven and changed by individuals down in the organization many times over the years. These individuals influence by their personal power as opposed to position power.

I remember a discussion during the time that I was working for Dow in Europe. My boss at the time was Peter Berner. Peter was terrific; extremely enthusiastic and motivating. I loved working for Peter. This period was a time of cost cutting and personnel reduction. Reducing headcount was necessary, but in some cases, the downsizing was handled very poorly by some leaders in the company.

Peter said to me, "Sam, I think Dow has lost its heart with the way the company is treating people." I smiled and responded, "Peter, do you think you've lost your heart?" He looked back at me with a puzzled look, "No, I don't think so." From that response, I said, "You definitely haven't and always treat people with respect." I continued, "Do you think I've lost my heart?" Peter responded, "Absolutely not. But Roger (name changed to protect the innocent) definitely has. Look how bad he's treating his people." I agreed and we continued to discuss individuals that had and had not lost their respect for treating people.

We concluded that it's not the company, but rather, the people at all levels that shape the culture of a company. The key for each of us, with the right values and behaviors, is to exert leadership, do our best to influence others, and drive the company in the preferred direction.

Don't wait for others to take the lead. You have the ability in your own position to set a high standard and influence others. Set an example for others, conduct yourself with integrity and credibility, and continually push the organization towards excellence.

I had the privilege to work with my counterparts at other companies around the world. I worked with industry associations such as the American Chemical Council (ACC), American Fuels and Petrochemical Association (AFPM), American Petroleum Institute (API), European Chemical Association (CEFIC), National Safety Council and many others. These organizations provided a forum for collectively improving ESG performance across the industry.

Interaction with government agencies is vital. I initiated, negotiated, and signed, on behalf of Dow, the first OSHA Voluntary Protection Program (VPP) corporate national agreement in 2003. I always dealt with people in governmental positions from a position of strength, treating them with mutual respect, but not being subservient. They had an important job to do, and I had an important job to do.

One of the most recent and powerful industry work groups was the Process Safety Advisory Group which was co-sponsored by API and AFPM. Jerry Wascom, President of Refining and Supply for ExxonMobil did a fine job of leading the team. I was an active member along with executives from several other top tier companies. Our focus was on preventing process safety incidents across the industry. We drove considerable progress in areas such as developing industry standards, sharing best practices and lessons learned, hazard identification, site safety assessments, mechanical integrity, and human reliability.

In all of these such encounters, I was able to help drive improvement and learn from others—all with the spirit of protecting people. I continued to learn and develop my own approach to Operational Excellence and Goal ZERO. I never wanted to "reinvent the wheel," but rather build on my experience and the experience of others. Why would you ever want to work hard to develop something that someone else has already done?

From the very beginning of my stint as a global corporate leader, I always tried to never forget where I came from, specifically, my years of plant operation. I remembered the old saying that people joked about: "Trust me, I'm from corporate and I'm here to help." To counter this opinion, I never asked anyone to do anything that I wouldn't feel comfortable doing. It was important for me to present a sense of capability, confidence, and humility. I worked hard to help our employees to succeed and have pride in their work.

If you've read the book this far, you are obviously interested in improving personally and improving your organization. This chapter is about you, your values, your character, and some of the steps it takes to be a true leader at any level and drive change.

**GOAL ZERO NUGGET:**
*Growth and expansion should come **after** achieving Operational Excellence.*

# Personal Values

As I look back, my values were heavily shaped by my parents, my faith, the Boy Scouts, and my competitive spirit from playing sports. Values are embedded in each of us at a very early stage in our lives. I've always approached life with a goal to be honest, ethical, and to always do my best. I enjoyed my Boy Scout days and proudly achieved the rank of Eagle Scout. The Boy Scout Law includes quality values for anyone, and we always tried to live up to them:

> *A scout is: trustworthy, loyal, helpful, friendly, courteous, kind, obedient, cheerful, thrifty, brave, clean, and reverent.*

As I progressed through my career, I realized that Robert Baden-Powell, the father of Boy Scouts, should have added a 13th principle—Safe. Safety does not happen by accident but rather by deliberately thinking about it and being proactive to prevent injuries. This principle is a terrific one to instill in every young person.

My Boy Scout experiences taught me many lessons which remained throughout my life. One is simply to leave your campsite cleaner than when you found it. Don't make excuses if it's not clean when you show up. Just clean it up—just do it! This philosophy definitely applies to every workplace and in every environment. If something needs to be done, don't complain, just do it.

As we get older and progress through life, we face many challenges to our values. It's not easy at times and the choices we make have long lasting consequences. Our friends and people we work with face these same challenges, especially leaders of companies in responsible positions.

I'll tell you a story that was a turning point in my career. I was blessed as I began my career to have many superb supervisors and leaders. They were tough, challenging, and demanding, but we always performed our work the right way. We followed the Dow and legal requirements at all times. I was happy and proud at the time to be working for Dow Chemical.

After many years of operations management, I became the Environmental Manager for Dow's Texas Operations in

Freeport, Texas in 1994. At the time, it was one of the largest chemical complexes in the world with over 5,000 employees and 90 operating units. My predecessor told me that one of the most important aspects of my job was to manage risk. I didn't realize that one of those risks was legal compliance. Previously, I only knew one way, and that was full legal compliance. Well, it didn't take me long to understand what he was talking about.

One of the facilities was the Magnesium production unit. Magnesium is a lightweight metal used in aircraft and other applications. The plant had been constructed in six months during World War II for the war effort. I quickly learned that the unit had many areas of potential non-compliance with the relatively new Environmental Protection Agency regulations. The Magnesium plant had been constructed long before any of these new regulations were enacted. This non-compliance was contrary to everything I had been accustomed to.

At the time, the Texas Operations site was led by a four-member Texas Operating Board (TOB). After considerable thought, I went to the TOB that had placed me in the job. Being careful on how I addressed the issue, I reminded them that I was new in the job and asked their advice. I asked them, "What should be my approach if I were to find a plant with major legal non compliances, requiring potentially millions of dollars to remedy and possibly putting the plant out of business?"

To my pleasure, each member of the TOB adamantly said they expected full compliance with the law, no matter the cost or consequences. They showed strong leadership, integrity, and tone at the top. My predecessor had mistakenly thought that he was doing good by "managing the risk" of noncompliance. This experience pointed out how often disconnects exist between top leadership and people down in the organization. We began addressing the noncompliance issues head on resulting in the Magnesium plant closure within the next 2 years.

Throughout my 20 years of global leadership in major multinational companies, I came across many controversial issues. I always researched each issue heavily so that I was personally comfortable with the right position to take. I was never going to provide leadership for any products or operations that I felt would endanger employees or the public or damage the environment in an unacceptable manner. This stance took courage, perseverance, and considerable discussion on many significant issues; but my values, constancy of purpose, and strong executive leaders above and around me always helped to prevail. I rest well at night knowing that we did things the right way.

> **GOAL ZERO NUGGET:**
> *Be true to your values.*

# Integrity and Credibility

This section discusses the importance of your individual integrity and credibility. It doesn't matter if you are an individual contributor or aspire to be in leadership roles; integrity and credibility impact your reputation and have a significant impact on your success or failure. Your reputation is precious, so work on it proactively. The definitions are very important:

- **Integrity.** *The quality of being honest and having strong moral principles*
- **Credibility.** *The quality of being trusted and believed in*

The Code of Conduct in most companies has rules prohibiting acceptance of gifts or trips from contractor companies and suppliers. This requirement is to help prevent impropriety or the appearance of impropriety. A couple of years before I retired, I received a nice ice chest at my home from one of our very good service providers. It was valued at around $300. My initial thought was that it was a nice gesture and I could really put it to good use. However, I quickly decided that I couldn't keep the ice chest. I had a good relationship with the CEO of the company and I contacted him to say thanks but that I could not accept the ice chest and would return it to him.

We met and as I was moving the ice chest to his vehicle, I asked, "How many of these do you send out each year?" He replied, "I send out around 30." Then I asked, "How many people return them?" He smiled and said, "You're the first one. This says a lot about your integrity." I felt really good about what I had done. It's actually not difficult if you think about it. Why risk your job or potentially damage your reputation over a relatively low-cost item?

Truthfulness and honesty are essential. Many people get themselves into trouble because they don't want to deliver bad news. They tell "little white lies" or don't tell the whole story. Always remember that people get over bad news, but they never get over being lied to. Once you get a reputation for not telling the truth, you will have a very difficult time of rebuilding it.

A good practice is to always look at a particular situation from the other person's point of view. What information would he/she like to have and know about? Holding back pertinent information is often considered as bad as lying. We were always taught to be honest. Provide the bad news and full story right away, and then get on with correcting the situation.

Do what you commit to do; such a simple statement that is often not followed. If you commit to a certain action with your boss, make it a high priority to get it done. If he or she asks you several times if the task has been done, you are already in trouble.

Be competent at what you do. Too many people try to get by and fake their way. Most people can see right through this charade. Whatever your line of work, learn everything you can about your job and become an expert. I spent hours in each of my manufacturing plants learning every piece of equipment, lines, valves, and process technology. I knew my plants backwards and forwards.

Be principle focused, especially when making decisions. People often make a short-term decision that they later regret. If you face a difficult decision, don't just take the easiest path. Consider the impact the decision will have on your reputation and ensure you will be comfortable with the decision. How will you feel later when you look at the decision in your rearview mirror?

Finally, as a leader, I always tried to be as honest with our people as I possibly could. Honesty made my job easier because I never had to think back about what I had told them the last time we were together. Sometimes, of course, you have confidential information that you can't divulge. In these situations, you simply say that you can't talk about it at the current time, but never lie to your people. Tell the truth, do what you say you are going to do, be trustworthy, increase your competency, and remain genuine. All of these qualities will serve you well.

> **GOAL ZERO NUGGET:**
> *Your reputation depends on integrity and credibility.*

# Passion

I heard a story long ago that illustrates the importance of passion for your work. Oscar and George were maintenance workers for the railroad. One day while they were working on the railroad track, a car drove up and John, the CEO of the railroad, stepped out. John knew George very well, and they began talking about old times. After the CEO left, Oscar asked in amazement of how George knew the CEO of the company. George told him, "John and I started working together in maintenance many years ago. However, there was one major difference, it was just a job for me, I was *working for $2.50 an hour*. John, on the other hand, was *working for the railroad*. John had passion for the work he was doing and did everything he could to help make the company better from the very beginning. He loved his work and did whatever it took."

John is the type of person you want in your organization. Find people that don't just approach their work as a job. Find and develop those that demonstrate a daily drive to take ownership and make the workplace better. People that you have to constantly push certainly don't have the passion you are seeking.

Passion for work is when you can't wait to get started every morning. Passion for your family is when you can't wait to go home at the end of the day to be with them. When people have passion for something, they will do whatever it takes with persistence and enthusiasm. They create a sense of "flow," which I will describe later in this chapter. Whether you are performing a task, leading a project, running a department, or you are the CEO; do it with passion.

Every results focused leader I know has passion for what he or she is doing. These leaders have a vision, are decisive, and are willing to make tough decisions. Passion for achieving excellence is contagious and is an effective enabler. Passionate people drive culture and culture drives behavior. Passion leads to so many terrific results: pride in your work, self-satisfaction, self-esteem, and successful outcomes. People without passion don't do great things. Whatever you do, do it to the best of your ability, and always do it with passion.

> **GOAL ZERO NUGGET:**
> *Be passionate with your life's activities.*

# Courage

Around three weeks after I became Vice President of EH&S at Dow, our CEO scheduled a meeting to approve the purchase of a production plant from another company. Typically, we used meetings such as this to assure all details had been addressed and everyone was in alignment. In preparation for the meeting, I met with our EH&S due diligence team for an update on their due diligence of the acquisition.

To my disappointment, the due diligence team stated that the plant had reactors which had stress corrosion cracking. Stress corrosion cracking can lead to sudden and unexpected failure. At Dow, we would have never operated equipment in such a state. To complicate matters, the population surrounding the plant had been moving closer to the site over time.

The due diligence team said they had communicated this defect to the commercial team in charge of the acquisition, and the commercial team said they had committed money to replace the reactors. However, the timeline for replacement was over a year.

Prior to the executive leadership meeting, I met with the Vice President of the business who was in charge of the deal.

In our discussion, I told him I couldn't support the acquisition and operate the plant with the reactor in the current state. He believed that adding money into the budget to repair the problems was good enough. He was extremely furious and said that we had come this far and couldn't stop now. Despite his pressure, I told him that I was going to voice my opinion in the upcoming meeting.

During the executive review meeting, I explained that I had just become aware of the deal and was informed about the stress corrosion cracking issue prior to the meeting. From my experience, I wouldn't operate the plant in such a manner and have the risk of catastrophic failure with potentially serious consequences to the safety of our employees and the public.

To my surprise, my comments were the first time the CEO and the Vice President of Manufacturing had heard about the issue. The Vice President of the business said that we were getting the plant for 50 cents on the dollar. I said that I wouldn't take it for free and that's probably why it was being sold so cheap. The selling company obviously understood the risk. In the end, we stopped the deal and didn't make the acquisition. Following the meeting, the CEO told me, "This is why we put you in this job." Incidentally, the plant was never sold and was shut down by the owner and dismantled a short time later. The important learnings from this experience were:

- *You must have **courage** to speak up, even when you are the lone voice in the room on a particular issue. Never remain quiet if it threatens your integrity. These jobs are not a popularity contest.*
- *We obviously had **flaws in our due diligence process,** with the commercial organization driving most of the process. Issues such as the stress corrosion cracking should have been elevated to the appropriate decision makers much sooner in the process.*
- ***Scorecards** can sometimes drive the wrong behavior. Even though the Vice President of the business knew about the safety concerns, his scorecard was to grow the business. Checks and balances in an organization are important and powerful.*

# Don't Hesitate to Be Bold

*"Try and fail, but don't fail to try"* - **John Quincy Adams**

As a young engineer in research at Dow, I was working with a team focused on Toluene Diisocyanate (TDI) technology. TDI is used in the production of polyurethanes, primarily for flexible foam applications including bedding, furniture, and carpet underlay. TDI is also utilized for coatings, sealants, adhesives, and in transportation applications to make automobile parts lighter. This product leads to improvements in vehicle fuel efficiency and energy conservation.

Dow purchased the TDI technology and had just commissioned a new production plant. My department was conducting research on improving yields of the reaction of toluene diamine and phosgene to produce TDI.

The reaction technology involved a large, wiped-film mixer that was a huge energy user and a maintenance headache. While we were conducting pilot plant runs on various incremental improvements, we had an idea for a different approach involving high pressure, liquified phosgene. We believed this new technology could eliminate the need for the wiped-film mixer, prevent plugging, and lead to much higher yields. However, this technology entailed a major shift from the existing technology.

We conducted numerous technology reviews during those days. One frequent attendee was Levi Leathers, a member of the Dow Board of Directors. He was a much older gentleman (at least it seemed like that to me at the time) that had retired from Dow as the Executive Vice President of Manufacturing. Levi had a huge reputation across the company as a tough, smart leader that was very demanding.

I presented a summary of our current research during one of our technology reviews and concluded with future plans. I described our "long-term" plan to evaluate the new liquid phosgene concept. Levi became interested and asked if I thought it would work, and I answered that I thought it would. He growled as usual and said to move the project up on the priority list and work on it immediately. "Why wait?" he asked. Levi's direction was all it took for our top management to quickly get on board with their support.

To make a long story short, the new technology was a huge success. The wiped-film mixer was eliminated, and the yield increased significantly, generating millions of dollars in increased profit. This new technology was so different from the previous technology that I'm not sure we would have ever tried it if Levi hadn't pushed it through.

The point of this story is to be bold and take reasonable risks based on the data at hand. Many breakthrough ideas never get implemented because people are too conservative and reluctant to take risks. Another lesson is how much influence a board member or executive leader can have on a young person in an organization. Be bold!

# Proactive vs. Reactive Behavior

Leaders and employees have many competing priorities for their time. We've all heard the concepts of important and urgent. People may be well aware of items that are important to the organization but the urgent items commonly get the most focus. I'm going to generalize, but most people operate in either the **proactive** or **reactive behavior** mode pertaining to Operational Excellence.

I'll begin with the **reactive behavior** mode. Leaders rightfully spend the majority of their time on the high priority issues of the day. These activities may consist of major projects, change initiatives or responding (reacting) to crisis situations that may arise. Reliability, quality, and safety don't receive much attention when operations are going well. Leaders say the right things but the organization picks up on their lack of intensity and acts accordingly. Low consequence incidents or near misses don't receive much attention. Reactive behavior mode people don't increase their level of seriousness *until* something significant happens such as a fire, explosion, serious injury, impact to the environment, major non-compliance fine, or a significant quality event with a customer. If such an incident occurs, reactive behavior individuals turn all their attention to managing the incident. By then, it's too late.

I've seen manufacturing plants operate with a frequent number of minor leaks and spills. Reactive behavior leaders don't take these incidents too seriously *until* one of the spills becomes very large, ignites, and a major process safety incident develops. It's not unusual for major process safety incidents to result in several hundred million dollars of damage and business interruption. Some companies operate with a high number of relatively minor injuries or allow non-compliance with safety rules *until* one of the incidents results in the ultimate incident; a fatality to a friend and co-worker. Many companies conduct business with a regularity of minor customer quality complaints *until* one of the quality incidents results in millions of dollars in damage and loss of a large customer.

I see this kind of reactive behavior on the highways every day. People drive too fast or tailgate too close. They don't give themselves time to react if something goes wrong in front of them. These people don't think about the severe consequences of a major auto accident. They don't get serious about safe driving *until* an accident occurs. As a result, approximately 40,000 people lose their lives in U.S. traffic accidents each year.

The behavior mode practiced by the best Operational Excellence leaders is the **proactive behavior** mode. Proactive leaders maintain a good balance between the urgent and important activities. Proactive behavior leaders, like reactive behavior leaders, focus most of their time on the top priority items (which includes Operational Excellence). Proactive behavior leaders make a big deal out of seemingly small incidents and defects and set extremely high expectations for Operational Excellence at all times. They know and understand that attention to the smallest details is important for achieving Operational Excellence. I personally always drive progress the hardest when times are good—my philosophy is to challenge during good times and support during bad times.

You must focus on your urgent items, that's understood. However, you must also expect and insist that the people in your organization drive relatively minor incidents and non-compliance with requirements to zero in order to prevent any one of them from becoming major. It's your choice as an employee or leader in the organization, you can be **proactive** with a Goal ZERO approach to the smallest of details for

Operational Excellence, or you can be **reactive** and spend your time and money responding, investigating, and managing the impacts of major incidents and defects.

# Modest and Humble

A year or two after I began my career with Dow, I was assigned a project to lead the design, construction, and operation of a small pilot research unit. Our research group in Dow's Texas Operations had a small number of in-house contractor craftsmen that performed work for various projects.

After completing the design of the unit, I worked with one of the contractors, Ted, as he built the pilot unit. I was naturally proud of it, the first one in which I had primary responsibility. Several of us were talking in the control room about various projects and then it was my turn. I talked about the pilot unit that "I had built." Ted was there and started laughing and said, "Sam, I don't remember seeing any wrenches in your hands." He caught me off guard and I was a little embarrassed.

Ted was right, I hadn't physically built the unit or even designed it totally by myself. Ted had physically constructed the unit and I had received considerable help and advice from my supervisors on the design. I made it a point from that moment on to say "we" instead of "I" when talking about work activities, projects, and accomplishments. Most of the things we do involve some amount of contribution from others. Ted taught a valuable lesson to me that day which has remained ever since.

I still hear people overusing the words "I" and "My" in the work environment. I heard a CFO talking recently about "my budget" and "my financial reports." Everyone knows he didn't create them alone and it just doesn't sound right or come across well to others. Think about how you speak and give credit to others as much as possible.

*GOAL ZERO NUGGET:*
*Be careful saying "I" and "my."*

# Communication

Effective communication is essential for establishing and nurturing the culture you desire. You must spend a considerable amount of time listening, teaching, and communicating with your workforce. Two-way communication is vital. Communicate regularly and clearly both upwards and downwards in the organization. Take enough time to help people understand "why" something is important.

Effective and efficient communication is imperative because people are busy and have an enormous number of items competing for their attention. Strike a balance between communicating enough and not overloading the organization. Don't overcommunicate like so many retail organizations do by sending an email every day. I delete those immediately when I see them.

I always included a representative from our communications department as a member of my leadership team. I wanted the communications department to understand our actions to drive Operational Excellence performance and why this work was so important for the success of the company. Through their active participation, we provided an unlimited amount of material for companywide communications which helped in creating the culture and driving the behaviors we desired.

Communication upward to your supervision is as important as communicating with the people in your organization. I always took the approach of wanting to make my boss successful. It was important for me to understand what was important to him or her and for them to know what was important to me. Ensuring good alignment builds trust and clarity on priorities and objectives. Communication clarifies how everything fits into the big picture and helps create a productive relationship with each other. There should never be any uncertainty between someone and his/her boss or direct report. Keep your boss informed to build trust and ensure an aligned approach toward the important objectives of the organization.

Here are a few recommendations I believe will help improve the effectiveness of your communications.

- ***Be sincere, honest, and direct.*** *It's hard to regain credibility once you lose it. Always tell it like it is and don't sugar coat. When a problem arises, acknowledge it, but then spend time talking about the actions you and your team are taking. People are smart and know when a person is not being honest. And one selfish motive is: if you are always honest and consistent, you don't have to spend any time trying to remember what you said the last time.*

- ***Develop a communications plan.*** *Create a schedule to prevent too much time elapsing between messages and utilize various methods of communication: face to face, email, videos, webcasts, and social media.*

- ***Communications department.*** *Communications departments in larger companies are always looking for new and interesting items to communicate. Make it a point to have a communications specialist assigned to your department or function and keep them supplied with materials to help achieve your objectives. Communications personnel can be a major factor in helping to drive the culture that you want.*

- ***Constancy of purpose.*** *In his book, Out of the Crisis, W. Edwards Deming discusses the need for constancy of purpose. I couldn't agree more. Take your time to establish simple and easily understood principles and stick with them. Repeat them over and over. Nothing is more useless than flavor of the month programs.*

- ***Utilize different sources for communication.*** *The CEO, leadership team members, site leaders, and others should all share in communicating key messages. Mix it up.*

- ***Keep the audience in mind.*** *Remember, it's not about the message we send; rather, it's about how our audience perceives it.*

- ***Simplicity in writing.*** *Keep your written communications clear and easy to read. The Flesch-Kincaid Reading Ease method is extremely helpful (see Chapter 6).*

- ***Say it 10 times.*** *I'm a strong believer in communicating a consistent message and repeating it often and in different ways. Many people send out a single communication for a change initiative and believe everyone "gets it." That's hardly the truth. Many times, in my career, I witnessed someone hearing a message for the 3rd, 4th, or 5th time before the light bulb finally went off. Perhaps the person had other things on his/her mind and wasn't truly listening earlier. You must catch the receiver of your messages in the right frame of mind at the right time.*

- ***Eliminate confusion.*** *Casey Stengel, a right fielder and manager, best known as the manager of the championship New York Yankees of the 1950s, once said to his team, "All right, everyone, line up alphabetically according to your height." Leaders unknowingly create confusion at times by the way they communicate. Be sure your messages are clear and don't get misinterpreted.*

- ***Technical writing is different than writing a novel.*** *In my college English literature classes, the professor constantly instructed us to elaborate more, stretch out the verbiage and extend the use of vocabulary. My technical communications class, on the other hand, emphasized shorter sentences, elimination of unnecessary words, consistency in choice of words, and bullet points. Both styles have their place, so be sure to understand your audience and choose the appropriate style.*

- ***Quarterly webcasts.*** *We were diligent about conducting a quarterly broadcast for people in our global function. Quarterly seemed the right frequency and provided an excellent opportunity to communicate results, recognize good performance, and emphasize areas needing focus. Gaining alignment of your team is critical. If you have operations in the Asia Pacific region, conduct a special broadcast at night. Scheduling a meeting at a convenient time for them, when they are fresh, shows that you care.*

- ***Make it persuasive.*** *I learned long ago to make every communication persuasive. Whenever you communicate, don't just make it interesting. Take the opportunity to always include action statements for the organization. Never pass up an opportunity to persuade others.*

- ***Watch the harsh words.*** *We all get frustrated at times. It's best to sleep on it before lashing out at someone or sending a harsh email. A friend of mine told me that saying something you regret later is like squeezing toothpaste out of a tube. Once it's out, you can't get it back in!*

> **GOAL ZERO NUGGET:**
> *Communicating change—*
> *say it 10 times.*

# Terminology

One of the important elements of companywide communication is consistent terminology. As we all know, endless synonyms exist in any language and all serve their purpose. However, in business and in large organizations, establishing a consistent set of key terms to use for important concepts is critical.

For example, in this book I use the terminology Goal ZERO. It's written in a very specific manner and it is used the same way around the world. It doesn't matter what terminology you use, be consistent.

Reading books such as this one and attending conferences are important for learning new concepts and stimulating thoughts. That said, you must guard against people, after reading a book or attending a conference, from introducing new conflicting terminology at a single location in the organization. You will never drive Operational Excellence and achieve consistency if each location defines key concepts its own way; forever changing. Encourage people to bring back good concepts and potentially blend them into your existing systems and terminology.

This consistency in terminology is especially critical in global organizations where English is not the native language. People in those countries may have some English capability but their vocabulary is probably limited, just as your vocabulary would be in speaking a second language.

I could share stories about major disagreements, debates, and endless discussions simply because people had different interpretations for the same word or concept. This confusion happens among people with different native languages and even with people that speak the same language.

A simple example is "work process." Hearing the words, some people instinctively think of detailed process descriptions with swim lanes, while others may think of a simple one-page flow diagram or everything in between. Words and clear definitions are extremely important in any organization.

The bottom line is to standardize the key high-level terminology used in your organization, define it clearly in a glossary and be disciplined about everyone using it. This simple step will help keep people on the same page, reduce confusion, and enable faster progress.

# Time Management

Time is the most precious commodity we have. We each have 24 hours per day, 7 days per week, and 52 weeks per year—no more, no less. Properly managing your time and protecting the time of others is essential. If you haven't done so recently, I encourage you to refresh yourself from one of the many self-help books or classes on time management.

One tip is to constantly keep your strategy and priorities in front of you and stay focused on doing the most important work that will have the most impact on results. Don't let other people fill your agenda with low priority items. Minimize the length of meetings. A good administrative assistant is worth his/her weight in gold.

My schedule was continually packed. To save time, I often utilized "the power of 15 minutes." An example, if Susan wants to discuss a topic, I will often give her 15 minutes for the meeting. If she is really organized, she can state the problem, say what she is doing about it, request what she needs, and get some quick feedback in 15 minutes. Try it—you'll be amazed.

I remember a time management class in which the discussion turned into how often you call your mother on the telephone. Many people said they had a hard time finding the time to do so. The instructor said to change how we described the situation. He said, "If you haven't called your mother for a long time, tell her you haven't called because everything else is more important." He was right. I could never tell my mother this, so I always made it a priority to call her regularly!

# Life Balance

You hear a lot of talk about work-life balance. I prefer the words life-balance since work is such a big part of everyone's life. It's important to approach work in a positive manner and with life-balance. It's not just a job, but rather a career and something you should look forward to as part of your life.

Having said that, there is an essential need to maintain overall balance in your life. One of the models I have followed for many years is the Seven Fs. The Seven Fs come from a good book by Justin Belitz, *Success: Full Living*. The Seven Fs are:

1. *Faith*
2. *Family*
3. *Friends*
4. *Finance*
5. *Future focus*
6. *Fitness*
7. *Fun*

Faith, family, and friends are obvious and the most important in my opinion. Finance includes managing your money so you can provide for your basic needs. Finance includes the need to work since most of us weren't born rich. Future focus involves planning, goal setting, and constantly checking that you are on the right path and living your life as you want to. Fitness includes exercise, proper nutrition, sleep, and your emotional state. And fun; we all need it.

The philosophy is to not neglect any of the seven for very long. There will always be periods of time when any one of the seven dominates. Work may dominate for a while due to a special project or other consideration. Family may dominate at times for a number of reasons. The key is to maintain balance over the long term and make sure you are living up to the values and priorities you have for yourself.

I always worked very hard; no one ever challenged my work ethic. I worked many nights and weekends, but I also used all of my vacation each year. I always found that spending time away from work in the other Seven F categories, actually made me much more effective when back at work. My terrific wife, Stephanie, helped to maintain the balance in our lives.

One story involves my son, Brandon, as he was turning five years old and beginning to play baseball (tee-ball at that age). I loved sports and spending as much time with Brandon as possible, and I was always planning to coach his baseball team. However, his age for beginning baseball came at a time when I was working in a manufacturing plant with considerable problems, and we were working late every day. I faced a huge dilemma since I had always planned on coaching, but at the same time, I was needed at work.

I had always promised myself to put my family before work. So, after a lot of deliberation, I went to my boss and explained the situation. I told him I had decided to coach which would require me to be at practice and the games on some days at 4:00. I also said I would do whatever it took for the plant which included coming back out to work after practice or games as needed.

To my pleasure, he agreed and said I was doing the right thing. I coached Brandon's teams for nine straight years and enjoyed every minute. And our production plants didn't suffer since I had such a strong sense of ownership and did whatever it took. Of course, I didn't sit around watching much television during those years. You have to prioritize what you do with your time.

I've used this example many times through the years when young people told me they didn't have time for their children's activities. They were always surprised and glad to hear my story. You have the time; we all have 24 hours a day. How you spend your time depends on your priorities and effective time management.

Colin Powell is an American politician, diplomat, and retired four-star general who served as the 65th United States Secretary of State. He summed it up nicely, "Have fun in your command. Don't always run at breakneck speed. Take leave when you've earned it; spend time with your families. Corollary:

surround yourself with people who take their work seriously, but not themselves, those who work hard and play hard."

Your health, energy level, and fitness are extremely important. It's difficult to be an effective leader if you let your health decline. Take time to exercise, eat right, and get enough sleep. It's not one or the other, but all of the above to maintain peak performance.

Stress is something we all live with. We need a certain amount of stress to keep us motivated. I always found that I was more productive during the week when I had to get up early for work, rather than on a weekend if I didn't have anything scheduled on a Saturday morning. Stress can be a good thing.

However, we all need to be cautious of going over the break point such that stress overwhelms us and we get stressed out. It's different for each individual. Keep a watching eye for your personal stress overload just as you do for those you work with.

**GOAL ZERO NUGGET:**
*Maintain balance in your life.*

# CHAPTER 4

## A Passion for People

My grandpa used to tell stories to me about the changes that occurred during his lifetime. He'd talk about his first exposure to the television, the telephone, the airplane, electricity, and running water in his home. I used to think he was old since those conveniences seemed normal to me. And of course, he always reminded me, "He had to walk to and from school, barefoot in the snow, and uphill in both directions."

I guess that I'm getting to the old category myself (Taylor and Henry, my grandchildren, remind me of it frequently). In my freshman Chemical Engineering class at The University of Texas, our widely popular professor, Dr. John J. McKetta, told us to buy a good quality $30 slide rule because we would use it the rest of our career. Little did he know that the handheld calculator would be introduced a few years later.

In our early days at work, we carried beepers so that we could be reached. When the beeper went off, we had to find the nearest telephone and call in. Beepers lasted a few years and disappeared as mobile phones became commonplace.

Global communication took weeks or even months to occur. Telephone lines across the ocean were available but service was poor, and a trans-ocean conversation was very expensive. Today, we watch live broadcasts from anywhere in the world and talk to each other as if we were in the next room. Other inventions such as the internet, email, and social media have changed the way we all work and live. It's amazing that so many aspects of our lives have changed in a relatively short time. Technology is improving daily, and future changes will be mind boggling.

People, however, still have the basic needs that they've always had. Sure, we have the different demographic groups: Baby Boomers, Generation X, Millennials, Generation Z (Zoomers), and Generation Alpha (those born after 2010). Each generation grows up with the technology of its era. My grandchildren are Generation Z, and they were comfortable with their electronics before they could even read or write.

Organizations can have the best management system and processes available; but, without competent and motivated people implementing the system, nothing will get accomplished, and you won't win. Successful leaders understand these needs and have mastered the art of motivation and bringing out the best in their people. It all begins with leadership!

The previous chapter was about you as a leader. This chapter focuses on your ability to influence others. The success of any organization begins with leadership and tone at the top. How many times have you seen an organization that is not performing right, and a new leader comes in and quickly turns things around? It happens all the time at all levels in an organization: CEO, corporate staff, business units, site, and functional leaders.

People want to follow leaders who are honest, competent, future focused, visible, and inspiring. A good leader doesn't do it all himself or herself, but rather leads and creates an environment where the team achieves more than they ever dreamed possible.

Companies spend a lot of time and energy designing, installing, and maintaining their assets. Technical people love this aspect of the business and employ countless metrics to monitor equipment operations and efficiency. The people component, however, is much more abstract, challenging, and rewarding.

Leadership at all levels in the organization is a prerequisite to achieving excellence. All leaders, employees, and contractors must be committed to achieving excellence in every aspect of performance. Results focused leaders set high expectations, hold people accountable, and provide feedback on performance. Leaders must operate with the highest principles of integrity, ethics, and corporate responsibility. Competent and motivated people are required to operate assets and execute the system. Any company can have good equipment and strategic plans, but the winning companies develop a culture in which their people thrive.

Winning leaders instill winning attitudes in their people. Richard Denny, the author of *Motivate to Win*, listed 10 differences between winners and losers:

1. *A winner makes mistakes and says, "I was wrong."* A loser makes mistakes and says, "It wasn't my fault."
2. *A winner credits his good luck for winning even though it wasn't luck.* A loser credits his bad luck for losing, but it wasn't luck.
3. *A winner works harder and has more time.* A loser is always "too busy", too busy staying a failure.
4. *A winner goes through a problem.* A loser goes around it.
5. *A winner says he's sorry by making up for it.* A loser says he's sorry and does the same thing next time.
6. *A winner knows what to fight for and what to compromise on.* A loser compromises on what he should not and wastes time on trivial matters.
7. *A winner says, "I'm good but not as good as I ought to be."* A loser says, "Well, I'm not as bad as a lot of other people."
8. *A winner looks up to where he is going.* A loser looks down at those who have not yet achieved the position he has.
9. *A winner respects those that are superior to him and tries to learn from them.* A loser resents those that are superior to him and tries to find fault.
10. *A winner says, "There ought to be a better way of doing it."* A loser says, "Why change it, that's the way it's always been done."

My style as a leader was to be a "player coach." I always felt I was one member of the team even though I might have been the boss. My job was to be a catalyst for innovation and creative thoughts to drive improvement. I believed every member was important and critical for our success and I always wanted his or her honest input. By empowering the members of our team, it made it easier for me in the long run, which in turn always led to more successful outcomes.

My most important advice is be yourself and develop a leadership style that feels natural. Some people try to act differently as a leader than their natural state off of the job. This difference causes stress and doesn't typically turn out well. Be yourself, be authentic, and be consistent. People have good intentions, but they need guidance and leadership. Provide them with the skills, competencies, and tools to do their job with confidence and satisfaction. Continue to push responsibility to the front line by setting high expectations and empowering your people. Don't micromanage. People will respond enthusiastically and will deliver.

Successful leaders create alignment. They communicate clearly and often. People want to know "why" something is important and, "What's in it for me?" Take time to engage with your employees and listen to concerns. Discussion and debate are healthy for people to understand philosophy and direction. Help people understand the big picture and how their work impacts overall results. Leadership is most essential when things don't go right and when problems need to be overcome. The good leaders help their people remain calm and confident when dealing with adversity.

Building trust in the organization takes time. You must gain trust in your people and they need to have trust in you as their leader. Trust begins with a clear understanding of expectations and regular communications. Allow the people on your team to solve their own problems and then praise them for it. Empower them to make decisions within an agreed upon framework or limits, and make sure they know that you will have their back if things go wrong.

Help, encourage, and expect people to be their best and improve every day. Each person should take ownership and remember that he/she is the face of the company to others. Motivated people are terrific ambassadors for the organization. He/she should do whatever it takes to exceed customer's expectations. Create a workplace environment that is exciting and optimistic. Pride in the company is contagious. By doing so, you will have an organization in which people are proud to work and others want to join the team.

Results focused leaders may deliver results in different ways, but everything they do falls under the concepts of motivating people and of passionate execution of a management system, whether they call it that or not. They establish clear expectations, choose the right team members, develop and execute strategies and plans, instill consistent work practices, measure results, motivate people, and hold them accountable.

The culture that develops in a company is critical in driving consistency and long-term sustainability; but don't try to overdo it. In a large company, local cultures in different countries and at different locations are strong and will dominate. Your approach to developing a consistent company-wide culture should be to enhance the local culture with a few, critical expectations that people can understand. Having and enforcing a strong Code of Conduct is essential. A succinct Operational Excellence management system that is practical and not overbearing provides the framework. A Goal ZERO philosophy changes the way people think. Goal ZERO is an expectation for perfection that translates well globally.

I used to love when CEOs of our contractor companies would tell me that they could see a consistent Goal ZERO culture and approach at every one of our operating sites. They would hear and see the same things from people at the sites as they heard from us at corporate. They heard and saw the same message of excellence everywhere they went. That's a consistent and winning culture!

The examples I described are results of effective change management. Change management requires strong leadership, an inspiring vision, a sense of urgency, and constancy of purpose. Change management leadership is not a popularity contest. When you are driving change, some people will love what you are doing, and others will hate it. Many people naturally don't like change; however, keeping people future focused on the target works wonders in motivating teams.

Bringing your organization along together during times of change and giving people an opportunity for input will help to gain understanding and support. Frequent communication of all types is extremely critical for good leadership and to establish alignment through the organization. People tend to accept change much better if they understand "why" it's being done. Don't expect your people to understand with the first communication that goes out. Repeat the key messages over and over in various formats.

As I approached my job with global Operational Excellence, evaluating our site managers around the world and providing input to their line managers took much of my time. I clearly knew that we needed to have the right leader at each manufacturing location if we were going to meet our Goal ZERO expectations. Needless to say, we made a number of changes resulting with a final group of world-class plant managers. My evaluations also applied to the EH&S leaders at each site. The right person in the right job has a major impact on performance and morale. If you know that a leader is not getting the job done, move quickly to improve or replace the person. After making a change, most people will say they wish they had done it sooner. Don't delay.

One of the most important aspects of leadership is the ability to influence the behavior of others. Through the years, I spent a considerable amount of time exploring the concepts of behavior management. It's a challenge to motivate individuals across diverse organizations to align on common themes and perform to their highest potential. Our successful outcomes were the result of creating the right environment so that our people could win.

For years, I have enjoyed a quote by Pat Riley, a five-time National Basketball Association championship coach. He described his job as a leader perfectly, "I am a management person. My job is to create an environment where my players can flourish. They are the ones that truly get the job done. I do what I can, through organization and guidance, to put them in a position to be successful. I am at my best when I am of service to them. Not subservient, but of service. As much as I can, I remove my ego. In the long run, I know that I will benefit from their success as much as they do. It is the same for all managers."

Influential leadership at all levels in the organization is important to drive change. Here are some of the topics I will cover in this chapter regarding results focused leadership:

1. **Culture.** *An organization's culture serves as a guideline for expectations, behavior, beliefs and motivation.*
2. **Building a winning organization.** *Hiring the right people, preparing them for success and delivering on high expectations exemplifies high performing teams.*
3. **Getting the most out of your people.** *Motivated people on a winning team achieve more than they ever dreamed possible.*

4. **Driving improvement.** *You should expect and achieve continuous and measurable improvement in performance at all times.*
5. **Change management.** *Most people don't like change, but leaders can employ effective ways to achieve change successfully.*
6. **Behavior management.** *The Goal ZERO philosophy has a significant impact on individual behavior.*
7. **Learning.** *Ensure that training and learning are effective and efficient.*
8. **Communication.** *Communicate in a manner that is clearly understood by your audience.*

# People Strategy

Most organizations have many types of strategies: business strategies, growth strategies, etc. How many organizations actually have a people strategy? I'm talking about a comprehensive, fine-tuned approach to achieving your people objectives. A good people strategy covers the entire life cycle of the people management process: talent identification, recruiting, hiring, employee and leadership skills development, getting the most out of each person, performance evaluation, motivating the organization, and succession planning. You won't achieve excellence in your organization if you don't have competent, reliable, and motivated people. Successful implementation of a people strategy creates a winning culture with 100% of the people aligned, on board, and executing to their highest potential.

The importance of the human factor for achieving Operational Excellence cannot be overemphasized. I contend that every organization should include a people section in its management system that they continually execute and improve. Your people strategy should begin with a clear vision, desired outcomes, and a set of objectives for people leadership and development. The strategy should include clear responsibilities and accountabilities for individuals, leaders, the human resources function, and the company. It should also include the various human resources work processes for achieving the desired results. Finally, the people strategy should include important metrics that are tracked and monitored regularly to monitor progress.

It's important to develop and document your system for people leadership and continually improve it. Begin with your key objectives and then ask important questions such as:

- *How do we manage our recruiting process?*
- *How do we achieve diversity and equality?*
- *How do we train new people and is our training efficient?*
- *How do we evaluate performance of individuals and leaders?*
- *How do we recognize and reward good performance?*
- *How do we compensate people and does this compensation plan drive desired behaviors and achieve intended results?*
- *How do we identify future leaders?*
- *How do we give future leaders unique developmental opportunities?*
- *How do we perform robust succession planning?*
- *How do we motivate people to do their best?*

I'm sure you can add many additional questions to the list. Once your list is complete, document the processes utilized to address each of the questions. Regularly review the effectiveness of these processes and whether they are achieving the desired results with your people. Keep it simple; these processes should not be complicated.

Without such a system, the emphasis on certain areas of people leadership can rise and fall over time or even fall through the cracks. Approaches to human resources processes might change every time a new leader comes on board. Leaders won't understand how the various elements impact each other and you will never achieve consistency.

Line leadership has the primary accountability for the people reporting to them. The human resources department has the accountability for developing and driving work processes that deliver measurable results in individual performance and leadership. The desired approach is to be best in class in people leadership with a management system that the company uses, continually gets improved over time, and delivers results.

The people element is one of the most significant factors in achieving Operational Excellence.

> **GOAL ZERO NUGGET:**
> *Include a robust people strategy in*
> *your management system.*

# Individual Ownership, Accountability, and Responsibility

One of the most important elements of a Goal ZERO culture is to establish a high level of individual ownership, accountability, and responsibility in every person across the organization. Of course, system improvements can and always should be made; but every person should focus on what he/she individually can control and his/her individual behaviors.

Earlier, I discussed the benefits of an Expectations Document for the organization. One of the first elements of an Expectations Document should state the following:

> *Leaders, employees, and contractors are responsible for*
> *meeting applicable company rules and requirements, working*
> *safely, avoiding mistakes, identifying hazards, preventing unsafe*
> *work practices, and reporting unsafe conditions.*

This statement may seem obvious. Tragically, terrible incidents often occur simply because someone hasn't followed a rule, procedure, or paid attention to detail while performing a task. Communicate this expectation and discuss it frequently with your work force. A good management system builds on previous successes and failures. Each and every individual must perform up to expectations and not repeat the same mistakes of the past.

Develop a culture in which individuals ask themselves, "What can I do to make things better?" and, "What can I do to make this job successful?" Following an incident, the pertinent question is, "What could I have done to prevent the incident?" The emphasis is on "I" as opposed to blaming someone else.

Taking ownership is essential. Develop this expectation from the beginning for new people. The first few hours, days, and weeks for a new employee or contractor are the most influential time for establishing an understanding of expectations and your culture.

One of the simplest examples of the importance of "I" is someone walking down the hall and slipping on a banana peel. Sure, someone should not have left the banana peel on the floor — an issue that should be addressed, but don't blame others. The person who fell should be on the lookout for banana peels on the floor and other hazards. Hazards exist all around us, and we must be proactive and responsible in addressing them in the right manner. One of our manufacturing plants had a mirror on the wall with an excellent inscription: **"This person is responsible for my safety."**

By creating a healthy culture of individual accountability in every person, and by not criticizing people for mistakes, people begin to take on more responsibility for their actions rather than looking for others to blame. Set clear expectations, offer public praise when people do well and address it quickly when they don't. If you treat people like adults, they will respond.

Each person in the organization must perform up to his or her full potential. It's very effective when every person in your organization can answer the question: "What are you personally responsible and accountable for?" Answers such as, "I help with", or "I'm part of," or "I assist with" are not sufficient. Your organization becomes much more effective when each person has individual accountability and works with a sense of ownership. Each person should be able to clearly state what he/she is accountable for.

Creating personal accountability begins with each position having a clear job description stating responsibilities. In the job description, be sure to avoid watered down verbs such as "help, assist, participate, advise, consult, etc." Instead, use action verbs such as "lead, manage, coordinate, etc." Make the responsibilities action oriented with well-defined deliverables. Be crisp and don't make it too long. Ensure that every person has an "active" role with responsibility in daily work, on projects, and on teams. These activities build commitment, a positive attitude, and pride.

If you supervise others, accept complete ownership and accountability for your team. Be strong and enforce compliance will rules and standards at all times. Be pleased with your team's progress but never satisfied with your current status. Give your team credit when things are going well. When things aren't going so well, don't blame others; take ownership, accept responsibility, and take action to improve.

> **GOAL ZERO NUGGET:**
> *Instill a sense of ownership in every*
> *person on the team.*

# Divide and Conquer

How often have you seen that most of the work and responsibility falls to just a few people? A few individuals step forward while others sit back and allow it to occur. I've seen it in departments, workgroups, and in teams. This imbalance of workload doesn't utilize every participants' time and talent and is not effective.

I've always kept a watchful eye for this type of situation and did my best to spread the load. I call this "Divide and Conquer." During my Boy Scout days, I was the Patrol Leader for our patrol. We attended various camporees where we competed with other patrols and troops. One of the events was communicating messages by Morse Code. Of course, this era was way before cell phones. Using Morse Code, you could communicate to others by using a flashlight or a flag. Each letter of the alphabet had a specific code, a combination of dots and dashes.

The competition consisted of dividing our patrol into two groups. One group was given several paragraphs of a message which they were to communicate over to the other group by flag signals. This communication was a huge challenge as it was extremely difficult memorizing the entire Morse Code.

To address the challenge, I created my first "Divide and Conquer" approach. Instead of each person trying to memorize the entire code, I divided responsibilities by having each person memorize only 10 letters and numbers. That way, we collectively had the entire alphabet and all numbers covered. Each scout did his part and accepted his individual accountability. The sending and receiving groups each operated as a TEAM. We were proud to win the event on a regular basis and every scout knew he had contributed to the team's success. None of us was as good as all of us.

In my global leadership roles, I always reminded myself that there were thousands of employees around the world and only one of me. Divide and Conquer works at any level and in any team; local and global. Make expectations very clear and hold people accountable. Push decision making down to the lowest level. Empower people within a defined framework and limits. They will rise to the challenge and will be much more motivated.

Focus as much as possible on individual accountability and be careful with "shared accountability." Shared accountability becomes fuzzy and too many important items fall through the cracks. Create a high expectations environment and most will succeed. For those few that don't, perhaps they are in the wrong job and a change is needed. Everyone must do his/her part and deliver on his/her accountabilities.

# Know Your People

As a leader, the people on your team want to know that you care about them and have their best interests at heart. I changed jobs often throughout my career and assumed leadership of many new teams. In doing so, I developed a simple introductory questionnaire to help speed the process of getting acquainted. I gave this questionnaire to the people of teams I inherited and to new people that joined my team. A sampling of the questions I would ask include:

- *Birthday?*
- *Family information?*
- *Personal background: where are you from, what are your hobbies, what are your outside activities, and other interesting things about you?*
- *What are your special work talents and interests that you have or enjoy doing?*

- *Which areas of our department and company do you feel are working very well or you are particularly proud of?*
- *Which areas of our department and company do you feel need focus for improvement?*
- *How can I best help you to be successful in your work?*
- *What would be your initial focus if you were in my job?*
- *Are there any additional comments, insights, or suggestions for me?*

People enjoy the fact that you care enough to ask these questions. If they didn't want to answer certain questions, that was perfectly fine. The answers provide you with valuable information for discussion that helps build strong relationships quickly. This information helps you to understand where the employee feels his or her talents are and how best to utilize them in the organization. And people always appreciate when you remember their birthdays.

# Culture

Culture in an organization develops over time and is highly influenced by leadership. We often joked, "What interests my boss, fascinates me!" Leader's behaviors and actions are an incredible force in creating a Goal ZERO culture. A Goal ZERO culture shapes the way people think and act. Goal ZERO serves as a way to express your combined expectations and values in a consistent manner—Goal ZERO performance, Goal ZERO behavior, etc.

Create a culture that brings out the best in people. Develop a culture of competent, motivated, dedicated, and loyal people. From my experience, the best company cultures have the following elements:

- *People feel they are doing worthwhile work.*
- *People feel appreciated.*
- *People feel they have growth opportunities.*
- *People like clarity; they don't like confusion and inefficiency.*
- *People understand their job responsibilities and the responsibilities of others.*

- *People are held accountable.*
- *People feel comfortable in delivering bad news.*
- *People follow the core values of respect, transparency, and ethics.*
- *People are motivated by the future focus of the organization.*
- *People say they work hard but also have never had so much fun.*
- *People like regular communications.*
- *People feel they are fairly compensated.*
- *People like to be on a winning team.*

Work hard to create an esprit de corps; a shared spirit of camaraderie, enthusiasm, and dedication to the organization. With the right culture, everyone gets better. "A rising tide lifts all boats!" Treat people with respect and keep them future focused. Create an organization in which people are lined up to enter instead of wanting to leave. Most important, keep it simple and make it a place where you are proud to work.

One important technique that companies use to evaluate the culture is to conduct employee engagement surveys. Surveys take considerable time and money and are typically conducted every year or two. These are normally administered by the human resources department. Many companies choose to use outside resources for the survey so that the company can benchmark data to prespecified, consistent questions.

The human resources department should request additional questions from other functions such as safety and Operational Excellence items. It's important to ask questions regarding work floor conditions, compliance, and willingness to report incidents. Include questions, as appropriate, from your Operational Excellence Expectations Document to make sure your people are actually following and meeting the expectations.

All functions should cooperate together in developing an engaged workforce and in driving excellence across the company. If you are going to conduct a survey, you should not waste the opportunity to make full use of it. And of course, you must be willing to act on the findings and communicate back to your workforce. The right culture is vitally important for achieving Operational Excellence in your organization.

# Transparency

Openness and honesty are vital in any organization. You want to know the problems so you can take action to improve. You must know about emerging issues and trends before they become more significant.

Transparency is essential in a Goal ZERO culture, but it is not achieved overnight. Rather, transparency develops over time and takes a considerable amount of trust. This openness is a challenge for cultures where people don't like bad news exposed, i.e., they don't want to air their dirty laundry. This reticence is especially true in certain countries of global organizations.

Transparency begins with setting clear expectations. In our company, we set the expectation that every incident needed to be reported and investigated as appropriate. When in doubt, report the incident. This practice prevents bad surprises later on. Reporting of high potential incidents is as important for learning as when something really bad happens. Reporting is the only way you can learn and make continuous improvement. Leadership at the highest levels should be fully aware of all significant issues.

Leaders at all levels play a critical role in establishing transparency. The objective is to learn from mistakes and problems, not to place blame. If someone reports a problem and then gets scolded or chewed out, human nature dictates he/she will be less likely to report the next time. Leaders need to remain calm when receiving bad news, respond in a professional manner and focus on improvement. Your response will impact the willingness of people in your organization to communicate bad news in the future.

The following story illustrates the importance of early reporting. Joe is a friend of mine who works at a major automobile manufacturing company. One day he called to tell me about a tragic incident that had occurred at one of their facilities in South America. An employee had punctured a drum of flammable materials with a forklift. The spill resulted in a fire that burned 75% of the person's body. The person died after 10 painful days in the hospital. Joe said that corporate leadership didn't hear about the incident until *after* the forklift operator's death.

During my discussion with Joe, we talked about the difference in transparency between our two companies. In my company, we discussed all global incidents, even minor ones, at every Monday morning Corporate Leadership Team meeting. At his company, the culture and behavior seemed to be quite different. Many incidents didn't get reported to headquarters until they became "very serious." I wondered to myself if this culture was one of the reasons his company was the subject of so many class-action lawsuits. Were problems kept at lower levels too long until they became widespread and out of control?

Another story on lack of transparency involved one of our company's manufacturing plants in China. We received a report through our employee hot line that there had been a coverup of an injury at the plant. We launched an investigation and unfortunately determined that an employee had cut his hand requiring sutures. The employee's supervisor and the EH&S manager decided to hide the injury and took the employee to a private doctor for treatment. Fortunately, an honest and concerned fellow employee reported the incident to leadership.

The female manager of the plant was extremely good and one of my favorite managers in China. We worked with her on the situation and decided to terminate the supervisor and the EH&S manager. We had high expectations for honesty and transparency and would not tolerate such a deliberate act.

A few weeks later, we received another employee hot line communication that the plant manager had actually been in on the incident coverup. The supervisor who had been terminated had met with the plant manager to discuss the incident and had secretly recorded the conversation. This recording provided all of the evidence we needed to confirm that the plant manager had sadly agreed to the incident cover up.

Of course, we let her go and lost a previously very good plant manager with high potential for this deliberate dishonest deed. It was difficult since the terminations left us without three key leaders in a relatively small plant, but we had no other choice. It was the right thing to do.

I made it a point to communicate these dismissals across our entire company. This incident was a teachable moment for all. I talked about our Goal ZERO aspirations for eliminating injuries, but that we wanted to accomplish our vision the right way, not by hiding injuries. We never took any action for someone experiencing an injury unless he/she deliberately violated safety rules. However, we made it very clear that we expected openness and honestly in reporting of all incidents so that we can learn, and failure to do so would result in serious consequences. I can assure you that everyone got the message and it was another step forward in establishing the culture that we wanted.

Companies must also be transparent with the public, especially in local communities where you operate. The longer that you hold onto bad news, the worse it gets. People get over bad news after the initial shock and, in the long term, respect the transparency. Be open and honest, and report incidents and problems when they occur. Take ownership and be responsible. Communicate the actions you are taking to correct the situation and prevent it from happening again. Honesty, integrity, and transparency will serve you well.

### GOAL ZERO NUGGET:
*Always communicate the bad news.*

# Sense of Urgency

I always worked to establish a sense of urgency among the people in our company. I was commonly known for saying "Go faster!" Results focused leaders constantly prioritize to determine the highest priority items that will make the most difference, and then get after it. When we decided in a meeting that something needed to be done, I often said, "This afternoon would be a good time to start."

It's important to continually prioritize and determine the actions that will make the most difference in driving desired results. Once prioritization is complete, develop a sense of urgency in your people to focus on and execute the actions for these highest priorities.

You never want the same type of incident to occur when it has already occurred in another area of your company or in another company. Learning from incidents and then rapidly implementing corrective actions are critical for preventing recurrence.

To add emphasis, we replaced the commonly used "safety moment" with a "sense of urgency" moment. We didn't require it for all meetings, but only when there was a current topic to highlight. Safety moments can quickly become old, stale, and ineffective. I've seen safety "moments" turn into a 15-minute discussion in an hour-long meeting. The safety topic had nothing to do with the purpose of the meeting. In the end, it took up a considerable amount of time that could have been used to address other, more serious issues.

A "sense of urgency" moment can deal with topics much broader than safety. It can pertain to a current incident that has occurred elsewhere and how it relates to your operation. A "sense of urgency" moment builds a sense of awareness in areas where the event didn't occur and helps spread the word. It stresses why it is so important to take action as quickly as possible. Shame on you if the same type of incident ever happens in your area before you have taken action based on a previous event elsewhere.

# Make It Fun

The workplace doesn't have to be serious all of the time. Think of creative ways to loosen up the organization in ways to help accelerate your agenda. Here's a story to illustrate the point. When I returned from Europe to Texas and became the EH&S leader for the Dow Texas Operations facility, the relations with the local unions had become somewhat contentious over the previous years. We began conducting numerous meetings with union leadership to discuss various issues of concern and rebuild relations.

One of the priorities for me was improving safety performance across the site of 5,000 employees and a considerable number of contractors. At the end of one of our meetings, I issued a challenge to union leadership that all of the union employees could not work the entire summer injury free.

Of course, everyone likes to take on a challenge, so the discussion became interesting. The union leaders proposed that if they worked the entire summer injury free, that company leadership would wash their personal vehicles at the company fire station. I countered and said, this sounds good, but let's do it monthly, June to August, and we will wash your vehicles each month if you work injury free. However, if there is an injury in a month, you will wash the leadership team's vehicles. They shook their heads a bit, but finally accepted the challenge.

It was amazing how their focus over the next three months shifted to making sure their people worked safely, which was exactly what I wanted them to do. The month of June ended as an injury free month. We went to the fire station and the union leaders were sitting on lawn chairs ready to watch us wash their vehicles, which were primarily trucks. They really enjoyed it, took a lot of pictures and we all had fun that day.

In July, a pipe fitter unfortunately experienced a finger cut requiring stitches. Now it was time for the union leaders to wash our vehicles. Again, we all proceeded to the fire station and just as they were about to wash our vehicles, they pulled out paper bags with the eyes cut out and put them over their heads. They said there was no way they were going to be seen washing management's trucks. We all got a good laugh out of that.

August turned out to be another injury free month and we gladly washed their trucks again. This entire three-month challenge turned out successful in many ways. Safety performance improved and sustained going forward. We all had a lot of fun and the entire site was interested in the monthly outcome. And our relationship with the union leadership improved immensely. It was truly a win-win situation. Make the workplace a fun place.

# Challenge During Good Times, Support During Bad

Everyone that works in operations knows that you can be on cloud nine as you drive home one day and as low as a snake the next. Nothing is better than when your operation is running smoothly and you are setting production records. On the other hand, when something breaks and the unit shuts down, the disappointment hits you quickly. Sometimes in extreme cases, the problems are serious or the cause unknown, and these are the worst of times as you and your team work to resolve the issues and get the plant back online.

Your job as a leader is to provide a sense of calm, confidence, and assurance to your team during such times. Shelter the heat from upper management pressure and provide a calming influence for your people. Your people have enough pressure already in dealing with the urgent issues at hand. They want to know that you have their back and will support them. Avoid panic and help your people to keep their heads straight so they can think clearly and do their best.

At the same time, people up the line which are responsible for sales, customers, and profitability naturally get concerned and want to know what is being done. It's critical to communicate proactively and regularly to keep everyone up to date. The last thing you need is unnecessary pressure from above during times of trouble.

As I moved into higher leadership roles, my philosophy was always to drive progress and improvement very hard when times were *good* and to be as supportive as possible when times were *rough*. I always remembered what it was like to be on the receiving end. I've had plenty of site managers tell me how much they noticed and appreciated the support during difficult times. Many leaders sadly take the opposite approach. They become complacent and take good operations for granted, and alternatively, become overly upset when there are problems. They are reactive, not proactive, as I discussed earlier.

My message is to be proactive. Drive Operational Excellence very hard and set high expectations during good times. Be as supportive as possible during the difficult times. Any manufacturing person knows what I'm talking about, we've all been there.

**GOAL ZERO NUGGET:**
*Challenge during good times,*
*support during bad.*

# Build Loyalty

When I had been working around three years for Dow, I managed a project to design and install some new process equipment into an operating unit. I was all in and loved the assignment. During the middle of the project, my father-in-law, at the age of 59, suffered a heart attack and was life flighted to Houston. We raced to the hospital and he was in critical condition for about two weeks before passing away. To complicate matters, my wife, Stephanie, was pregnant with our first child and delivered our new baby 10 days after her father died.

It was a traumatic time for us all. I spent 2 weeks at the hospital with Stephanie and her family. I kept my boss up to date with what was going on. I remember my two brother-in-laws saying they would use their vacation for the days they were not at work and I expected the same. It really didn't matter.

However, to my surprise, when I returned to work my boss said I didn't need to use vacation for the time off. I couldn't believe it and was extremely appreciative. I was already loyal to the company, but this action by my supervisor took my loyalty to a new level. I remember it still to this day and I paid Dow back countless times for all the nights, weekends, and long hours I gladly worked to help make the company great. Do everything you can to develop loyalty in your employees, it's incredibly powerful!

> ***GOAL ZERO NUGGET:***
> *Take care of your people*
> *and build loyalty.*

# Try to Say Yes

I was fortunate through my career to receive a considerable amount of excellent leadership training. At Dow, some of our sites were salaried operations and some had unions representing the hourly workforce. I enjoyed working in both types of organizations. In my opinion, people are basically the same and respond well to good leadership and attention. Of course, we preferred salaried operations to avoid the hassles if you have unreasonable union leadership. We had frequent training workshops on how to maintain a salaried operation. One of the principles was to take good care of your employees or else the union will.

In one of the early training sessions I attended, there was an ex-union negotiator named Ralph teaching a section of the course. Ralph was a tough guy and had a long history of giving companies a rough time. He worked for our company now, conducting training sessions. During the session, he asked us, "Which of you believe you are a good supervisor?" Of course, everyone's hand went up. Then he asked, "If a plant operator came to you and said his child had been run over by a car and he needed to go home, would you let him go?" We all raised our hands and said of course we'd let him go take care of his child.

Then Ralph posed a third question, "What if an operator came to you and said that his cat was feeling bad this morning, and he needed to go home to check on the cat?" Only a few of us raised our hands. That's when he became heated and challenged our supervisory and decision-making skills. The discussion became lively. Ralph said that we were passing our personal judgement on what was important to our operator. He said we should let him go home and check on his cat. Ralph's comments were very surprising to all of us.

As we continued the discussion, it became clearer that he was right. This cat may have been the highest priority in Ralph's life. Any pet owner understands that feeling. If it's important to your employee, *try to say yes* if you can. Your employee will be much appreciative and more loyal in the future. If you say no, he'll be bitter and remember it forever, and it will cause much more damage in the long-term than letting him go home in the first place.

On the other hand, maintain a watchful eye on each of your employees. If a person starts to abuse a privilege such as this, you'll know he's playing games and you should approach him differently. You can never allow your willingness to say yes get out of hand. Just don't punish the entire group for one or two bad actors.

The point of this section is that the natural tendency of many leaders is to immediately say no to suggestions. However, be careful and give the request or suggestion some thought. If something is very important to your people and it's a reasonable request, try to say yes even though it's not important to you. You will be delighted at how positively people react.

# Motivation

A favorite story of mine is about a plant control board operator named Harry. Harry was a smart guy, but typically did the minimum and was never proactive. A supervisor would tell him to make a process change so he'd do it and then sit back down. Harry was seen by others as a mediocre performer with little enthusiasm.

His supervisor, Robert, went bowling one night with some friends. As he entered the bowling alley, he heard someone yelling on the far-left lane. It was Harry! He stood there and watched Harry as he bowled. Harry couldn't wait until his turn to bowl. He'd get up excitedly, grab his bowling ball, and give it his total concentration. Then he'd roll the ball down the lane, watching intently. As the ball struck the pins, he'd jump for joy and shout out. Robert had never seen this side of Harry; how could it be the same person? How could Harry act so differently at work from the way he did at bowling?

With bowling, you hear the sounds and see the pins as they get knocked down. It's immediate feedback on your performance. You record your score which creates an element of self-satisfaction. You constantly try to get better and improve your performance.

In contrast, imagine the game of bowling if there was a soundproof curtain in front of the pins. You roll the ball down the lane and it travels under the curtain. You don't see or hear anything. You don't keep score. You just sit back down and await your next turn. That would take all of the excitement out of the game and that's how Harry felt at work

The difference is feedback. Harry was not getting feedback at work regarding the company or unit performance, and the results of his actions. If you want your people to be excited and enthusiastic about their work, give them constant feedback about their individual performance and the performance of the unit, department, or company. Show them the score. Feedback is the breakfast of champions.

> *GOAL ZERO NUGGET:*
> *Provide constant feedback on individual*
> *and organization performance.*

# Flow

The book, *Flow—The Psychology of Optimal Experience,* by Mihaly Csikszentmihalyi, is one of my favorites. The theme in the book is about the essence of life. The author describes a state of mind called *"Flow"* in which time flies by. We've all experienced it. How many times have you been doing something that you love, and you look at your watch and realize how late it is? People will spend all night enthusiastically working on their favorite hobby. On the other hand, we've all been in a boring meeting where the minutes and seconds drag by, thinking that the meeting will never end.

The author outlines his theory that people are happiest when they are in a state of *Flow*—a state of concentration or complete absorption with the activity at hand and the situation. It is a state in which people are so involved in an activity that nothing else seems to matter. The Flow state is an optimal state of intrinsic motivation, where the person is fully immersed in what they are doing.

Csikszentmihalyi performed research with thousands of people trying to determine what creates the state of Flow. Of course, it's different for different individuals. Results showed that activities such as hobbies, sports, sex, and a challenging job can all create Flow.

The secret is to find the activities you love the most and create Flow in your life. You can even adapt your activities, such as your work to create Flow for yourself and for your team. As a leader, make it fun, make it a game, create challenge, and recognize accomplishments. These actions can help create Flow. All of the people I worked with understood the concept of Flow and we worked hard at it and loved it.

# Future Focus

One of the Seven Fs that I described earlier in this chapter is to be future focused. It's important for individuals and for teams. By being future focused, it helps to put today's problems and challenges into perspective and creates hope and optimism.

When we moved to The Netherlands for my European expatriate assignment, our son, Brandon, was 13 years old. We were leaving the town where he was raised and had lived all of his life. He had many friends, enjoyed hunting and fishing and played lots of sports. Life was good! The first few months in Europe were challenging. Although he was excited about the European experience, I could tell he was a bit depressed at the big change that had taken place in his life.

The Antwerp International School that he attended was terrific and the school had many activities for the students. We traveled extensively which Brandon really enjoyed. My job was director of process engineering and process control for Dow Europe, which required considerable travel. Brandon was able to come along at times and visit new places. However, there were also slow days in which there weren't many activities.

To help Brandon become future focused, I bought two items to pin on the wall. One was a European map that we could write on and wipe off. The second was a year-at-a-glance calendar. We got together and began discussing our plans for the future. First, we put his school activities on the calendar, which included his sporting event trips to neighboring cities such as London, Hamburg, and Paris, all cool places. We added home trips back to the United States. Then we spent time marking the map for these trips and deciding where else to take additional trips. We'd agree on a plan and add these to the calendar.

Eventually, Brandon became so interested in the future that he would look months ahead and ask, "Dad, what are we going to do on this weekend?" He was excited and wanted to fill the entire calendar with activities. Getting Brandon future focused changed everything and he thoroughly enjoyed our 2 1/2 years in Europe.

Sports teams are the master of future focus. Their game schedule is well-defined and excellent coaches motivate their teams to give their best to win. By being laser focused on the future, players work extremely hard to get in good shape and perfect their skills. They may lose a particular game and it's easy for the team to get depressed. However, the sun always comes up the next day, and by the coach keeping them future focused, the players bounce back and focus forward rather than on the past.

Low morale in organizations has often been the result of poor leadership and lack of hope for the future. Paint a bright future, create optimism, and approach work with enthusiasm. Enthusiasm reflects confidence, spreads good cheer, raises morale, and helps to inspire others. Generating enthusiasm within yourself is an important first step towards success. Everyone is attracted to the magnetism of enthusiasm. Keep your people future focused and you will enjoy the results.

*GOAL ZERO NUGGET:*
*Motivate people through future focus.*

# Teams—Confidence in Self / Confidence in Others

Teams are an essential aspect of any organization. A model I learned some time ago was a grid with "Confidence in Self" on the X-axis and "Confidence in Others" on the Y-axis. The ideal state for a high-performance team is to have high confidence in both categories. If you have a strong team in which individuals each have self-confidence and confidence in others on the team, there is no limit to what the team can achieve.

For teams at higher levels in the organization, there typically isn't a problem with self-confidence. Individuals have been successful in their careers and have made it to this level.

Confidence in others, however, is often a challenge. If you have a team of self-confident individuals that don't have confidence in others, there will be a severe lack of trust.

In your various approaches to team building, keep this concept in mind. Confidence in others is built in many ways. Confidence in others comes when team members are competent, honest, take responsibility for their mistakes, meet their commitments, and are willing to step up and do whatever is necessary.

Bruce Piasecki, in his book *"Doing More with Teams,"* makes some excellent observations. Piasecki states "One way in which teams are magical is that they allow all types of individuals to succeed. People who would not normally be able to succeed on an individual basis can reap the benefits of success and reach peaks they would not be able to climb alone."

Some team members may be planners, other may be doers, and still others may be natural born leaders. "The planners and doers are often people whose creativity and contributions may go unnoticed because they do not have the internal spark to market themselves or stand out like the natural born leader. Nonetheless, the mix of differences meld, and as the group comes together, the team becomes one as it triumphs." Piasecki got it right. Understanding each other and respecting each other's talents goes a long way towards building confidence in self and confidence in others.

# Friendly Competition

By now in the book, you know that I place a lot of value on competition. I believe a good competitive spirit and a desire to perform well and win is extremely motivating. Of course, you can overdo competition and it can result in unintended consequences, so manage and monitor competition carefully.

People figured out long ago that competition helps sports to be more interesting. Enormous benefits are derived from playing sports. You get plenty of exercise, you learn about the importance of teamwork and you learn to execute your individual responsibilities. When every member of the team does his/her part, it's terrific to see it all come together.

Keeping score and competing is much more exciting than just participating. College football stadiums attract 100,000 people for games on weekends. I wonder how many people would attend if the two teams just played a game without scores—like a scrimmage. I believe there would be a lot of empty seats. Every team begins the year with enthusiasm, wanting to win the championship. Results are posted each week providing the top teams with pride and the lower teams with incentive to do better.

Why shouldn't the same concept be true with any organization? In business, the external competition is easy to identify and there are numerous ways to measure and compare performance. Competition and keeping score motivates us all to do better. Everyone on the team should know the score and how the team is doing. Nonprofits should use the same concepts. Look for specific things you do, stakeholders you care about, and identify your "competitors." You may not be competing with them directly, but you can benchmark and compare specific activities and results for best practices. A competitive spirit is good for the people in an organization. Benchmarking and taking action to improve is always helpful.

Friendly competition is also helpful within an organization. We used to compare performance results of our operating locations on all types of parameters. We felt that if each of them was working to be best in class, we would be in good shape as a company. I used friendly competition frequently between countries where we operated. I enjoyed going into a plant in Texas and highlighting how the French were doing something better than they were. I was probing into their competitive spirit and pride. Then I'd go to the same French plant and find something the Americans were doing better and challenge them. It was always fun and it worked.

As with any good intentions, there can be unintended consequences. Intense competition can motivate people to drive reporting underground. Keep the competitive spirit positive and with the purpose of motivating everyone to do better. Leadership and culture are the keys to openness and transparent reporting.

Competition yields many benefits. Competition teaches us to put forth our best effort and helps us to learn to win and lose gracefully. Nobody likes a boastful person, and nobody likes a whiner or pouter. Competition gives us the opportunities to cope with feelings of pride and disappointment and to learn to process them in healthy ways. Competition helps us to learn to cope when things don't go our way. Competition helps people to try harder and helps to build self-esteem. Learn to utilize competition effectively.

# Hire, Develop, and Inspire

Some human resources organizations define the employee life cycle as hire, develop, retain, and offboard. I've always had a problem with the word retain when it comes to people; the definition of retain is "to keep in one's possession." I don't like the idea that I am being retained. Instead, I like to replace retain with the word inspire.

Do everything possible in your company to excite your employees about their jobs and the future. Create the environment in which they enjoy coming to work every day and are passionate about helping to make the company better.

Developing an excellent employee value proposition is one way to inspire people in the organization. The old question is always true, "What's in it for me?" Create an employee value proposition so there is no other place he or she would rather be. You want a company where people are lined up to get in. Inspired people brag to others about your workplace. Take care of your people and they will take care of the company.

The war for talent is real. Every organization needs talent and every competitor is searching for the same type of individuals. You need outstanding people in order to achieve Operational Excellence and win. Hiring skilled talent is especially important when working with hazardous materials such as the industry I worked in.

Hiring the right individuals is the most important function a leader performs. I personally put a tremendous amount of effort into recruiting; making sure we were doing a good job of identifying talent, personally interviewing thousands of individuals, making sure we selected the right ones and then making sure they got off to a good start for a long, successful career. I always wanted to make sure individuals had the right technical skills, the right social skills, and would be the type of person we would enjoy working with.

Why would someone want to work at your company? What do your facilities look like? What are people's first impression when they set foot on your property? Why would someone want to stay? What would make someone want to leave? These are all important questions to address. If you make these a priority, you will be far ahead in not only making your company attractive for recruits, but also for your existing employees.

> **GOAL ZERO NUGGET:**
> *Inspire the people in your organization.*

# Identify the Talent in Your Organization

An old saying is popular about what it takes to become a professional golfer. All it takes is good technique, determination, lots of practice, and God given talent! There isn't much we can do about the God given talent we were born with so most of us will never become a professional golfer. However, almost everyone has some type of skills that need to be recognized and utilized.

I've seen many new leaders in an organization quickly change almost every person on their team. They are looking for people that fit their mold and their expectations. They lose years of experience in the process. They often let their search for perfect get in the way of good. I've seen many of those same leaders fail and/or take longer to make progress.

I assumed leadership of many teams throughout the years. One of my first priorities was learning about my people as well as I could rather than making rapid changes. I wanted to know the skills they thought they were good at and how they brought value to the organization. I often found many of them had years of valuable experience in the department or company and some of their unique talents had been overlooked. I appreciated the past contributions they had made and the potential of their unique value. I clearly understood that none of us was as smart as all of us.

Some individuals were superb leaders. Others were individual contributors: competent, reliable, and consistent performers that constantly delivered on their commitments. Some were outspoken and critical, but I appreciated their input, as long as they were positive in speaking up and not constantly complaining. A few were exceptionally creative, typically a little different from the mainstream conservative types. I called these "stallions" and tried my best to harness their talents into making the organization great. I loved people that were proactive and self-starters; I enjoyed saying "whoa" a lot better than "giddy-up." Some team members didn't live up to expectations or were detrimental to the organization and I didn't hesitate to quickly make a change.

Each team I managed ended up different than the one before. I believe that with this approach and playing to each person's talents, we always came up with a diverse, high performing team that drove rapid transformation. All these people needed in most cases was good leadership. The bottom line is not to overlook the hidden talents your people may have and do your best to capture and utilize these talents for the benefit of your organization.

# Recognition and Appreciation

I am a strong believer that feedback is the breakfast of champions. People want to be listened to, trusted, given responsibility, and thanked for a good job. Everyone enjoys a pat on the back or an occasional thank you. I've often told our leaders that we don't have a budget for giving out praise and personal recognition. It's so easy to do and yet so underutilized.

I often wrote personal handwritten notes of appreciation when I saw someone doing something special. On one occasion early in my career, we had an operator named Gary who had been a problem performer just a year earlier. He was beginning to show excellent initiative, so I wrote a letter complementing him on some of his specific contributions and his value to the team. During a visit to my parent's home a month later, my mother showed a copy of the letter to me. I asked how she had obtained the letter. She said Gary had been so proud of the letter that he sent a copy to his mother. She in turn, being a proud mother, sent copies to her two sisters, one of which lived in the same town as my mother. Her sister knew our family and gave a copy to my mother. It was just one example of how much impact a simple note of sincere appreciation can have.

On another occasion, I had taken over leadership of our Polycarbonate Production Plant at Dow. Polycarbonate is a high-quality thermoplastic used in a wide variety of applications such as DVDs, bullet proof glass, automobile applications, electronics, appliances, and even the clear front cover on soft drink machines. This production plant had considerable operational problems and it was a daily grind in the early days just to keep the plant operating. There was a lot of pressure from the sales organization and morale was extremely low when I arrived.

As we began to make progress, we decided to serve ice cream one day when we established a new daily production record. I wanted our people to know how much I appreciated their hard work and contributions. My boss happened to arrive while we were eating ice cream and told me sternly, "We don't celebrate daily records around here." I said, "Well, I do. We have to start somewhere." I can tell you our people appreciated the recognition very much and it helped to recognize the hard work they were doing.

Companies may have many established reward and recognition programs in place, but don't let that stop you from going further. Proper recognition serves so many purposes: it's meaningful to the team or person receiving the recognition, it serves as motivation to others in the organization and it doesn't cost much. Make sure recognition is sincere and given as immediate as possible. Be specific regarding the reason for the recognition and communicate why the accomplishments are valuable and important. As the American poet Maya Angelou once wrote, "I've learned that people will forget what you said, people will forget what you did, but people will never forget how you made them feel."

> **GOAL ZERO NUGGET:**
> *Everyone enjoys a pat on the back.*

# Spouses, Partners, and Families

Spouses, partners, and family members are extremely important in how well an employee functions. I always considered the family a part of our extended team. When there is trouble at home, it's constantly on an employee's mind. If you are having lots of problems at work and your employee is working long hours, it takes a toll on the family.

We always enjoyed conducting a family day at the plant. Before we began these, family members had no idea about the work of their loved one. We always received tremendous feedback when we held these events. You could see the pride in our employees' eyes when they showed their family where they worked and the responsibilities they had.

On one occasion, one of our control board operators, Johnny, was telling his wife about his work. He told her that he had to know everything about the plant and be able to respond to any of the hundreds of alarms that might activate. At first, she said, "No, I don't believe it." I replied, "Yes, it's true. Johnny oversees this entire control board." She was definitely impressed but was a little puzzled. She turned to Johnny and asked, "Then why do you act so dumb at home?" We all got a good laugh out of that one.

Finally, keep the children in mind. For any event, make a special effort to make it fun for the children. If you take care of the kids, everything else falls into place.

# Behavior Management

The only way anything gets accomplished in an organization is through the behavior of people. Whether you want to improve reliability, increase production, reduce quality defects, eliminate injuries, or take advantage of value creating opportunities, it is accomplished through the behavior of people. Employees need to do more of certain behaviors, less of other behaviors, or change their current behaviors. Therefore, one of the most important subjects for leaders to understand is human behavior.

Human behavior is one of the most studied concepts of all time. Why do we do the things we do? What drives us? When do our behaviors become habit? How much influence can we have on the behavior of others?

As a leader, create the environment so people conduct themselves ethically. You want them to work the right way even when no one is watching. You want them to comply with the Code of Conduct and follow rules and procedures. To eliminate injuries, unsafe behaviors must be eliminated. In short, you want predictable performance and confidence that your employees will do the right thing and make the right decisions.

Many books have been written on the subject of human behavior. One outstanding book written by Aubrey Daniels, is *Bringing Out the Best in People*. One of the behavioral models he describes is the Antecedent-Behavior-Consequence (ABC) model. His book has more detail, but I'll provide my simple summary.

The three primary terms used in the model are:

*A = Antecedent*
*B = Behavior*
*C = Consequences*

- *Antecedent includes conditions before we act, how we think, the rules, the expectations, the situation we are in and our past personal experiences.*
- *Behavior is the action we take: do we perform safe acts, follow the rules, and work with care, or do we perform unsafe acts, break rules, and take unnecessary risks?*
- *Consequences occur from every behavior; consequences can be positive or negative and intended or unintended.*

The ABC concept is quite simple and powerful. An antecedent comes before a behavior and a consequence is a result of the behavior. Our behavior is shaped by pre-existing conditions (antecedents) and by the potential consequences of our behavior (both past consequences and future potential consequences). Consequences of previous behaviors become antecedents for future behaviors.

An example of ABC is one of driving an automobile. My daughter, Sharon, loved her dance classes and I loved watching her. Let's assume a situation in which Sharon has a dance recital tonight; however, I am leaving work late and might not get to the recital on time. I have a choice regarding how I will drive (my behavior). The antecedents are that I am running late, I want to get there on time, I love watching her, I know the speed limit and I know roughly how much a ticket will cost if I get caught speeding. If I speed, I might make it to the recital on time (positive consequence for a bad behavior). However, I also might receive a speeding ticket and even worse, I might get involved in a traffic accident (two negative consequences to a bad behavior).

On the other hand, if I drive the speed limit, I know I will be late for the recital (negative consequence to a good behavior), but I won't get a speeding ticket and will reduce the risk of a traffic accident (two positive consequences to a good behavior). These antecedents and consequences will impact my decision making.

These are the types of situations and decisions we face every day. In the above example, the decision of my behavior to obey the speed limit or not will result in possible negative or positive consequences. Of course, a much-preferred earlier behavior would have been for me to have left sooner and not put myself in this situation to begin with. All behaviors have consequences, and consequences turn into antecedents for future behaviors. The cycle of ABC—ABC—ABC—ABC goes on and on and our behaviors get shaped by the antecedents and consequences we experience.

In your organization, it's critical to have antecedents in place such as clear expectations, a Code of Conduct, practical rules, easy to understand procedures and a Goal ZERO culture. Most companies are good at creating antecedents and letting people know what they want them to do; that's the easy part.

In addition to good antecedents, there also needs to be a culture of consequences. Most consequences in your organization should be positive for good behaviors and good performance (praise, reward, recognition, and thank you). Positive reinforcements are powerful. A frequent occurrence is when someone *does something good and nothing happens.* You'll often hear, "No one knows or appreciates anything I do around here. Why should I follow the rules, why should I go the extra mile?" Don't pass up opportunities to issue sincere thanks and appreciation (positive consequences) when you notice someone doing something right.

Effective leaders create designed positive consequences that then become effective antecedents. We always had effective recognition programs for production plants that achieved production or safety records. We made a big deal out of the recognition and communicated widely, showing sincere recognition to those that deserved it. This communication was a positive consequence for those that received the recognition, and it also served as a power antecedent for others to work harder to achieve the recognition the next time.

On the other hand, negative consequences are extremely important, but hopefully not used as often. In a Goal ZERO culture, you must never ignore or neglect to act when observing bad behaviors. Bad behaviors (unsafe acts, rule breaking, non-compliance, etc.) must always have consequences and people need to understand them. The consequence may be a quick intervention or short discussion. Negative consequences don't need to imply punishment. Remember, if you ignore bad behavior, that's a positive consequence to the person for a negative behavior and he/she is more likely to repeat the same undesired behavior again in the future. Put most of your energy into positive consequences, but don't hesitate to apply a negative consequence when needed.

The most effective consequences are those that are positive, immediate, and certain. People love "positive" reinforcement (a pat on the back) and recognition. Do it as "immediate" after the behavior as possible and be specific. Providing feedback to someone for something he/she did a year ago has much less impact than for something he/she did earlier in the day. And finally, "certain" means people expect consequences for particular behaviors. "Certain" consequences are a prerequisite for establishing a Goal ZERO culture. People know they will be positively recognized for good performance and behaviors and know there will be consequences for negative behaviors.

Culture and leadership are the keys. The culture of any organization definitely impacts the way people behave. A Goal ZERO culture (zero rule breaking, zero unsafe acts, etc.) will lead to Goal ZERO performance. The ABC methodology is an effective tool for helping in this area. There are consequences to every behavior, whether they are intentional or not. It's a sign of a poor leader when his or her people consistently don't follow rules or make poor decisions without consequences. By consistently applying the techniques of ABC and communicating clearly and frequently, people will understand the expectations within your organization and adapt accordingly.

> **GOAL ZERO NUGGET:**
> *Antecedents and consequences*
> *drive human behavior.*

# Training and Development

*"Train people well enough so they can leave,*
*treat them well enough so they don't want to."*
**– Richard Branson**

*"What if I train them and they leave?"*
*"What if you don't and they stay?"*
**– W. Edwards Deming**

Companies spend an enormous amount of time and money training its personnel. Employees must have the skills and knowledge to perform their job effectively. Far too many incidents occur in which one of the root causes is lack of adequate training.

Effective training is a challenge. I prefer to place the emphasis on learning as opposed to training, thereby focusing on the pupil rather than the teacher. A couple of techniques we have found to be extremely effective are chalk talks and competition.

You've all participated in your share of classroom training. The instructor is speaking, and the audience looks like they are barely awake, about to die from boredom. The minutes on the clock seem to be at a standstill. It seems like the people are being spoon fed, but don't want to eat. A similar situation is computer-based training, as people speed through the course to finish as quickly as possible. They check the box for the training, but do they really learn?

An effective technique is utilizing "chalk talks." For production plant operators, we put the emphasis on the operator to learn rather than for us to teach. The operator had a training schedule that included a weekly chalk talk to demonstrate his or her learning. The operator knew he/she needed to learn the material that week because he/she would have to present it at the end of the week. The process consisted of the operator drawing a portion of the production plant on the chalkboard and then describing the process and answering questions. Not only did this technique provide the student an opportunity to demonstrate what he/she had learned, it also provided coachable moments for areas in which he/she needed help.

It's amazing how this simple approach changed the behavior of students and the effectiveness and speed at which they learned. You could see the pride and confidence build as the person demonstrated his/her newly acquired knowledge.

We utilized another successful technique for more experienced personnel who attended training or workshops lasting several days. At the beginning of the session, we divided the students into teams. At the end of the course, the teams were expected to present an overview of a case study associated with the training material. The presentations were judged by senior leaders and the results were highly publicized. The teams worked on their presentations each day and night of the training course.

The energy level for learning was much higher since the participants knew they had to learn and present. More important, participants enjoyed the competition, which created a level of pride in their work. Try this in your companies and you'll see the difference.

# Getting Leaders Up to Speed Quickly

Manufacturing plant managers have a tremendous number and variety of responsibilities. Plant managers deal with technology, projects, reliability, budgets, communications, people, the public, and the safe operation of their facility. When a person is assigned a plant manager role, he/she drinks from the fire hose for the first six months or so, with so much to learn; and typically, the urgent issues of the day get the most attention. The danger in this is possibly overlooking some very important items, which may not be urgent at the time. Some companies have various types of good training and onboarding processes; while other companies simply tell the new leader to get on with it.

My biggest concern for any new plant manager was for the person to operate the plant safely. To help with this objective, we developed the New Plant Manager Review, a process for new manufacturing plant managers that can be implemented for any new leader. The primary theme of the review was process safety since the consequences of a major event can be so severe. We wanted each new plant manager to clearly understand the major risks at his/her new plant and to ensure proper precautions were in place to prevent incidents. However, the review was much broader and focused on understanding and execution of the plant's Operational Excellence Management System and achieving a Goal ZERO workplace.

We developed a list of items as a guide for the new manager's review. At first, our process safety experts got excited and wanted to develop training for these topics. But we said no, the intent is for the new plant manager to work with his/her team to develop the answers and presentation. The experts would be available as a resource if needed. The assignment was for the plant manager to give an interactive presentation within 90 days on the items listed. The audience was his/her team, a plant manager from another location, additional key leadership and a few subject matter experts.

The items the manager had to address with his/her team and include in the presentation were:

1.   *Overview of the plant management system*
2.   *Basic knowledge of the plant process*
3.   *Top risks and hazards of the process*
4.   *Approach to managing process safety hazards and risks*
5.   *Outstanding action items and mitigation risks*
6.   *Competency and experience levels of the staff*
7.   *History of incidents at the site*
8.   *Latest audit reports and action items*
9.   *Process Hazard Analysis (PHA) management*
10.  *Asset integrity of the unit*
11.  *Unique site or community issues*
12.  *Top 10 technology lessons learned that should prevent future incidents*

This New Plant Manager Review was one of the most successful activities we conducted for helping new plant managers quickly assimilate into their new job. By working closely with their new teams on an assignment with a deadline, they developed a close working relationship. In addition to the new managers learning how work was conducted at the site, they also were able to identify and correct any deficiencies in their management system before presentation time. The power was in the teams working together on the answers rather than sitting back and have someone teach them.

All managers that went through the process said it was tough, but well worth it early in their new assignment. Most of the plant managers implemented the same process for new direct reports they hired. I highly recommend this approach for bringing new leaders up to speed quickly.

*GOAL ZERO NUGGET:*
*Emphasize a person learning more*
*than the teacher teaching.*

# Bringing Out the Best in Functions

When I became the Vice President of EH&S at Dow, I found that many people in the function referred to themselves as subject matter experts and their job was to "help" the plants by providing tools, processes, advice, and tracking results. All were very good people, but I was surprised they were not held accountable for the resulting EH&S performance results and didn't believe they had the accountability. I commonly heard that the line is accountable for results (I agree) and the EH&S personnel were just advisors (I disagree on this notion). My question to the team was, "What if our tools, processes, and advice are not good and don't contribute to improvement? How will we measure the end result and our associated accountability?"

A common understanding in the industry is that an operating plant should not depend on the safety organization for its safety performance. The line leadership clearly has accountability for safety, not the function. However, many people in the function take this concept too far and begin to act in an advisory and consulting role. They say that if the line is accountable, then the function is not accountable. You can see this understanding in behaviors too; many will do their job in their allotted time, instead of a manufacturing behavior of doing whatever it takes, regardless of time, to achieve desired results. A huge difference exists between these two behaviors.

Based on my line leadership experience, I realized a change was necessary. I wanted each of our functional employees to have "skin in the game," so we added a strong accountability element for the function and each individual. To be clear, each individual manufacturing plant was clearly accountable for its operation and EH&S results, but I said the function's scorecard would include overall EH&S improvement for the company. If the function was providing the proper tools, processes, and support for improvement, then the measurable results needed to show it.

We eliminated titles such as advisor and consultant and changed to more action-oriented titles. These changes were a major shift in philosophy for the function in that they were being held accountable for bottom line EH&S results for the first time in their careers. Most people rose to the challenge. The increased enthusiasm in their behavior was evident. For the first time, they had a measurable scorecard that would show the results of their efforts.

All functions (EH&S, human resources, etc.) need to understand what success looks like and have clear accountability for expected results. I contend that in addition to providing the basic services of a function, these groups need an accountability element for overall results. Accountability provides a focus for driving improvement and creates a stronger function. Accountability also significantly improves morale. People enjoy being held accountable, working hard, and seeing the results of their work. Good people will respond well if they have the right work environment, incentives, and clear expectations.

Support functions need to maintain a good balance in their work; I call it "support and challenge." Individuals in functions need to provide support through their expertise, work processes, tools, and advice. Most people are very good at support and enjoy helping others. However, they must also have the courage to challenge the organization when necessary. Their added accountability for results provides them with "skin in the game" and lays the foundation for challenging the line. It's not enough to give advice like a consultant and then people in the line do whatever they wish. Functions need to do more, be strong, and not give up until the right actions are taking place. Persistence is key; functional people must create a level of discomfort at times to drive initiatives and the right behaviors. Of course, this role takes good human relation skills, but absolutely adds to effectiveness and credibility of the function and the results they will achieve.

Choosing the right leader for functions is critically important. Do you want a staff person to just manage the back office of a function; or do you want a strong leader to drive the function and achieve measurable improvement across the entire organization? There is a huge difference between the two. If the wrong person is assigned to lead a function with no history of driving bottom line results, then don't expect a paradigm shift in company performance.

A person with no proven history of influencing others and driving improvement will find it difficult to lead a function that has to work through influence of others to achieve results. The leader will do a good job of the basics; however, he/she might fall short in the skills it takes to improve company performance. A subject matter expert doesn't necessarily become a strong leader.

Just to be clear, line management should always have primary accountability for their people and performance of their organization. However, a terrific functional leader accepts accountability that his/her function's systems and tools are working well, and the line is delivering desired, measurable results. The right person in the job must influence others to achieve these results.

To all of you currently working in functions, you can control your own destiny for advancement. It's great if you want to be a subject matter expert in a particular field. However, if you want to become a leader, you must begin early to develop leadership skills and demonstrate a track record of ownership, passion, and results. Work closely with others to drive measurable results. You can gain these skills in a variety of manners such as through leadership development programs or leading teams and task forces. The key is to be seen by others as having the skills to lead and *influence,* then you will be an outstanding candidate for advancement.

My career took a major shift when I moved into a global functional leadership role. In prior roles, I always had clear line accountability with an appropriate number of direct reports and staff to do the job. In my new functional role, with only a small group of direct reports, I quickly realized I had to operate through influence of others to be successful.

An important success element was creating my "virtual" organization chart. In my mind, the CEO and his team "worked for me" for the purpose of promoting Operational Excellence and driving performance improvement. I felt that if I created an exciting and reasonable vision, strategy, and plan that was well understood, our people would get on board and execute. I needed leadership throughout the company to consistently deliver our message. I utilized every person in the organization who could help us spread the word and implement the programs.

I considered each of these people working for me in my "virtual" organization chart:

- *CEO*
- *Corporate leadership team members*
- *Board of Directors*
- *Site managers*
- *Site leadership team members*
- *Manufacturing*
- *Engineering*
- *Communications*
- *Human Resources*
- *Procurement*
- *Supply Chain*

If I could influence these people to align and work in the same direction, how could we fail? For example, I kept the CEO well informed and up to date, providing him talking points for driving the programs we were implementing and making sure he kept our messages front and center in everything he did. The phrase I used when working with him was, "Whatever interests my boss, fascinates me!" I always kept my boss and the rest of the corporate leadership team interested so they could keep their people fascinated!

The point of this section is that no one can accomplish results in a company alone. I hear individuals in functional roles often say, "I don't have enough resources." I find that to be a poor excuse. You have people all around wanting to do the right things. All you need to do is create the right vision and practical supporting programs, communicate well, and ask them (or tell them) what you want them to do, and they will deliver. At any level in the organization, you too can create your own virtual organization to accomplish your objectives.

**GOAL ZERO NUGGET:**
*You have more available resources
than you might realize.*

# Subject Matter Experts

As people progress through their careers, they advance as a single contributor or rise up the leadership ladder. The successful single contributors develop strong expertise in a subject and progress into roles with titles such as expert, scientist, specialist, technologist, or chief. These individuals are very important to the organization and are recognized for their individual knowledge and/or their previous contributions.

Line leaders get the most attention and direction from top management. Subject matter experts can fade out of sight, out of mind. Many of them are self-starters and will look for opportunities to improve the organization. Other subject matter experts who have developed significant expertise, but are a bit shy, tend to wait to be called when needed. They may become complacent and live on their reputation. These individuals need focused attention as well since they have such a high level of expertise and are necessary for improvement in performance. Keeping these individuals challenged and motivated to drive hard for improvement is vital for success. I've seen many subject matter experts become too comfortable in their jobs and develop a responsive mode, going wherever they are asked to present at meetings or whenever someone calls on them. I've seen many rest on their laurels from past contributions.

I remember one of our research scientists from Dow in my early years. He was a crystalline morphology expert. I saw him give the same presentation a hundred times over the years and always wondered what contribution he had made lately. A professional baseball player may have been the league's Most Valuable Player a few years earlier, but his contributions this year are what's most important. Why shouldn't it be that way in business?

Many techniques exist to keep these types of individuals challenged and on their toes. Keep them motivated and you will get much more value out of their contributions. Utilize techniques previously discussed such as ownership, individual accountability, responsibility, proactiveness, goal setting, and expectation of deliverables. Ensure a job description exists so everyone is aligned on expectations. The responsibilities should be action oriented and steer the specialist to drive towards intended results.

Job titles are important. I have never been a fan of passive job titles such as advisor and consultant. I always preferred titles with more teeth and ownership in them. A consultant provides help and advice but doesn't have ownership or accountability for results. Subject matter experts should be held accountable for broad performance trends in their area of expertise.

Subject matter experts should demonstrate ownership and overall accountability for their area of responsibility. This accountability gives them a healthy perspective for how to approach their job. The subject matter experts are not accountable for each individual workplace or location, but they should be held accountable for their particular expertise and how the company is performing.

The power with some of these individuals is the knowledge they have. Some subject matter experts are reluctant to document their knowledge or to share it widely with others. This behavior is not healthy. In a Goal ZERO company with a good management system, everyone must contribute to the success of the management system to continually improve.

In addition to performance improvement, subject matter experts should be recognized and rewarded for keeping the management system (standards, processes, procedures, training materials, etc.) up to date and effective. Challenge them, but then provide sincere recognition as appropriate. Technical professional individuals can be a major success factor in performance improvement of the organization.

# Fear of Losing Job

Many companies have been on an endless path of reorganizing, restructuring, and downsizing ever since the early 1990s as described in my history lesson in Chapter 2. Some companies never learn their lesson. During good times, they lose discipline and hire too many people. Then when times get tough, they are forced to downsize the organization and implement layoffs.

I learned early on to maintain the headcount of my teams on the lean side. People would come to me and say we needed more resources and I'd tell them, "No you don't, it's always better to stay slightly understaffed." They all learned to appreciate it when the bad times came around and we didn't need to do much cutting of budgets.

On one occasion, Dow announced there would be a reduction in headcount. After a few weeks, my best Instrument & Electrical Technician came to talk with me. He was shaking and said he was extremely worried about losing his job and couldn't sleep at night. I told him, "Danny, you are our best technician, and you would be the last to lose your job." He said he understood, but still couldn't get over the fear of the possibility. Some of your best people worry the most.

On many other occasions, I saw organizations take months to begin executing downsizing plans after announcements had been made. The pending employee reductions kept hanging over everyone's heads and impacted morale in significant ways. For the first time, some of the very best and loyal people updated resumes and started proactively looking elsewhere for a job. The damage was incredible.

Don't underestimate the impact that downsizing can have on the people leaving, but also on the people remaining. Avoid the need to downsize in the first place. However, if downsizing must be done, move as quickly as possible and communicate clearly as often as you can. Downsizing can be "slow and painful" or "fast and painful," so go fast.

> **GOAL ZERO NUGGET:**
> *Major change can be "slow and painful" or "fast and painful."*

# The Poor Performer

Many companies and leaders lack the skills for dealing with poor performers. These leaders let poor performance continue, resulting in morale loss with good performing employees and much worse, a significant incident as a result of the poor performance.

I've had my fair share of poor performers through the years. I'm proud that in most cases, I was successful in turning their performance around. I always approached poor performance as quickly and as directly as I could, time being of the essence. A poor performing employee needs to improve or move on. Most leaders will look back and wish they had moved faster to deal with a poor performer.

The biggest detriment of a poor performer is how much he/she negatively affects others in the workplace. When someone is not performing well, he/she knows it and everyone around them knows it as well. I focused on the best interest of the individual as well as the organization. Our work was too important to not have every individual pulling his or her fair share and contributing.

I always explained my expectations and where the person was falling short. Instead of focusing on the negative, I would say that I wanted them to succeed and clearly explained what had to be done to improve. I offered to help in any way I could. It was always important to get agreement and alignment, but that improvement needed to be made quickly. If the performance didn't improve, we'd conduct another session and tighten up expectations and timelines. Every step of the way, documentation of our discussions was important and applied to both union and non-union personnel.

In many cases, no one had ever been so clear and direct, which is a common problem with many supervisors. By making expectations very clear, most of my problem performers closed the gaps and significantly improved. However, in some cases, the person was a mismatch for the job and a change was necessary. Telling an individual about losing his or her job was never a pleasant experience, but employees often thanked me for everything I did for them. At least I knew I had done my best to help them succeed.

# Zero-Tolerance; Be Careful

In a Goal ZERO company, full compliance with all internal and external requirements is an expectation. The phrase is positive and the expectations are very clear. As I mentioned, ensure the rules are fair and reasonable and hold people accountable.

Many leaders like to use the words "zero-tolerance." I personally don't like the zero-tolerance terminology and never used it; zero-tolerance sounds like a threat and comes across negative. The phrase typically means automatic termination for noncompliance. Many types of consequences are available, short of termination, that are just as effective and are actually more powerful. Automatic termination limits your flexibility. Leaders use zero-tolerance as a simple way to deal with noncompliance and they want to send a message to the organization.

Many unintended consequences exist with a zero-tolerance policy. One of the biggest is the potential loss of a person with considerable valuable experience. If you use proper consequences the right way, short of termination, you can be assured the person will never repeat the same behavior again and will, in fact, become an ambassador to the organization for the importance of doing things the right way.

I'm not saying to never terminate individuals for poor behavior. Rather, make sure that termination is the right consequence for the particular individual and don't forget about the myriad of other potential consequences you have the ability to take.

# Goal ZERO—100%

Most people are good and will deliver on expectations if you communicate clearly and the culture of the company is one of Goal ZERO. However, a few individuals will always try to buck the system. Every person needs to be held accountable for following all rules and you must deal with the person individually if he/she doesn't comply. One note of caution, leaders' actions for dealing with noncompliance need to be seen as fair and just. Don't punish an individual if there is systemic violation of rules. If the people in your organization lose trust in leadership, they will not get on board with a Goal ZERO vision.

More importantly, a broad culture of rule breaking indicates a leadership and organization issue. It's a sign of poor leadership when an incident occurs and an individual is held accountable for breaking a rule, when the rule is broken all the time by others.

Here's a simple example to illustrate the point. I participated in hundreds of visits to operating facilities. My primary objectives were to interact with the people, communicate, learn, and see for myself how the facility was being operated. I tried my best to look for good practices and compliment people. People appreciated the recognition and sincere appreciation for the good work they were doing, and I received considerable positive feedback.

However, I never hesitated to address problems when I saw them. On one tour of a facility, our group went through a door with a sign that said, "Eye Protection Required." The group started entering the room anyway without eye protection. I stopped the group and asked about the sign. The leader knew he had made a mistake and nervously gave a weak excuse, saying, "We were just going in the room for a short time." I actually enjoyed these types of situations because they served as a coaching opportunity. I replied, "What kind of example does it set for others when leaders don't follow the rules? In a Goal ZERO plant, everyone must follow ALL of the requirements, ALL of the time. If the rule isn't important, take the sign down. It's that simple." Remember, the little things matter. Enforce ZERO rule breaking, ZERO non-compliance and ZERO defects until it becomes habit and culture. Goal ZERO—100%.

# You are My Ambassador

In my early years, I transferred to many different operating units within Dow's Texas Operations. I was always adamant about compliance and following the rules. I didn't want a single person to ever get hurt. However, I was disappointed at times to find a loose approach to compliance in new groups I joined.

I often heard the same excuse from supervisors for a particular rule such as wearing safety goggles in required areas, "We just can't get the operators to follow the rule." These were systemic and cultural issues that I needed to address.

So, I began what I secretly called my compliance ambassador program. I would begin by conducting an employee meeting to discuss our strategic plans. In the meeting, I'd make it crystal clear that I expected full compliance with all rules. We could change or eliminate a rule if we felt it didn't add value. Following the meeting, I'd send a note to everyone with a clear message about a particular rule in which noncompliance was common (such as required safety goggle areas). The note was important to document the communication.

I'd admit that we have not been in good compliance with safety goggle requirements in the past and why it was so important from a safety point of view to follow the rules at all times. I'd emphasize that we will never risk someone getting blinded by an unexpected release of a toxic, corrosive chemical. I'd say, "From this moment on, I expect full compliance with the safety goggle requirements in specified areas." It was always important to personalize the message and help people to understand "why" a particular rule was important.

I knew a single note wouldn't change everyone's behavior, so I asked my supervisors to watch closely and find the first person who breaks the rule (note, this is opposite from my typical approach of trying to find people doing something right). Due to old habits, it didn't take long before we'd catch the first person breaking the rule. As an example, I'll tell you how I would handle the situation with Charlie, who was first to break the rule.

The supervisor would tell Charlie that he needed to report to Sam's office at 3:00 PM to discuss the rule breaking incident. This delayed meeting notice was intended to give Charlie time to think about what he had done and for him to discuss it with the other operators. I wanted everyone to know the meeting was going to take place. By the time Charlie arrived in my office at 3:00, he would be concerned about what we were going to talk about and have his story all prepared.

I considered these opportunities as teachable moments and actually looked forward to them. My routine was fairly typical and I tried my best to urge the person to do most of the talking. In a very calm manner, I'd welcome him into my office, "Please sit down, Charlie." Charlie would sit and after a pause, I'd start the conversation, "You're one of our very good operators, but I understand you were in a safety goggle area today without goggles, breaking the rule. What do you have to say about this violation of the safety rule?" Charlie would squirm around and say something like, "Everyone breaks that rule all of the time." He'd make all kinds of excuses.

I'd say, "That's true, Charlie, our people didn't follow the rule consistently in the past. That's why I held the employee meeting and then sent the note saying that from now on, we are changing, and everyone must follow the rule. I am never going to allow anyone to get hurt by breaking a safety rule. Didn't you hear and read the message of full compliance?" Charlie responded, "Yes, but I guess I just forgot." I'd urge Charlie to say more about the incident. Then I'd say, "Charlie, have you ever given serious thought about getting blinded by a toxic chemical spraying into your eyes? What would it be like to never see your children again?" He'd think about it for a while and say, "I can't imagine anything worse."

Then I'd get more serious and say, "I can't take a chance with this kind of behavior anymore and risk that you might get blinded in our workplace. You know that I'm going to have to take some disciplinary action. This violation is so serious that I'm thinking about firing you for breaking the safety rule." Of course, this statement would be a shock to Charlie, and he'd say, "Please don't, I'll never do it again." Again, I'd remain silent by giving him time to think about it. Then after further discussion I'd say, "Well, how about some time off without pay? We have to send a strong message about compliance around here and that expectations are changing." Charlie didn't like that suggestion either and I'd give him more time to talk. Of course, by now Charlie was becoming very uncomfortable.

After enough deliberation, I'd make a suggestion, "Charlie, what if we don't do any disciplinary action, but you agree to go back to work and be my ambassador for full compliance in our plant? I am not going to tolerate non-compliance and we have to change our team's approach." Charlie, looking relieved, would say, "That's a great idea, Sam, and I'll do it.

I'll tell everyone. Thank you!" We'd shake hands and with a smile I'd say, "Thanks Charlie, I'm counting on you." After Charlie left, I would document the discussion and file in his records. Charlie didn't receive a lecture or punishment, but he surely didn't want to go through an uncomfortable discussion like that again.

The interesting part was that Charlie would then go out into the control room where his colleagues would be anxiously waiting for him. They'd ask, "What happened, Charlie? Did you get chewed out? Did you get any punishment?" Charlie, still a bit shaken and confused, would answer, "No, I didn't get chewed out or get any punishment, but I'm never going to break any rules again and you better not either. Sam is serious about safety and compliance."

I repeated this process many times in my career, stepping from one noncompliance item to another until we had the right culture of full compliance. This method works and is a positive way to address problems. The employee appreciates not being punished and we accomplish the intended results. There's something about the reverse psychology of a person being held accountable and not being punished, rather than resentful from receiving punishment. This technique gave terrific results and helped build the culture I was seeking. I always considered punishment as a last resort if all else failed.

# Retirement and Exiting Employees

I've always been a strong advocate of talking and listening to people in my organization to find out what's going on. People are willing to talk, but many people seem to open up a lot more when they are leaving the company.

I personally enjoyed visiting with individuals who were leaving. Not only was it an opportunity to thank them for their service, but I could solicit their thoughts for ways we could improve. Visiting with these individuals was time-consuming, but I learned considerable information, which was especially true when the exiting person was several layers down in the organization.

One example involved an operator in one of my early manufacturing plants. Our unit was located in a very large union site. Operators could bid for a job in a unit based on their seniority, work a minimum of two years, and then bid on another unit. When I began working at this unit, the problems were considerable, the morale was terrible, and there was fruit basket turnover of plant operators. I realized quickly that I had to turn this frequent turnover of personnel around and stop the loss of experience. We worked very hard on addressing operator issues. After a couple of years of improvement, I was proud of our accomplishments and the way the plant was operating.

One of our operators gave notice that he was going to bid on another unit, so I scheduled some time with him to ask why he was leaving. He said when he had arrived, the work environment was so bad that he marked his calendar to leave after two years; his mind was made up from the very beginning. I asked for specifics and he began to name his complaints. He talked about one of the front-line supervisors and how disrespectful he was. I said I agreed and I had moved him out 13 months ago. He named item after item, and it turned out we had corrected each one.

After a while, he had a puzzled look on his face and said, "I guess everything is better than I thought. I didn't realize how much things have improved, and I think I'll stay. I need to go talk to my co-workers about this." This conversation opened my eyes to the fact that people may not notice gradual change and you must communicate often to make improvement obvious to the organization.

HR departments typically conduct exit interviews, but the data is often lumped together and not as useful as it could be. Nothing is better than getting information directly from a person when he or she is willing to talk.

# Salaried Operations, Unions, and Works Councils

I've had the benefit and pleasure of working in locations of salaried operations, locations represented by a union and locations with works councils, primarily in Europe. I enjoyed them all. People are people and the same principles apply everywhere pertaining to honesty, respect, fairness and communication.

Most people are good, but you'll always find a few individuals who are difficult to work with in both union and non-union operations. It's not the system, but rather how your people are treated that makes the difference.

The origin of unions dates back to the 18th century in Europe. The purpose was to represent workers, protect their common interests and give them a stronger voice. Unions provided a check and balance with company management. Unions have helped all of us in many ways through the years such as negotiating wage increases, establishing reasonable work hours, gaining employee benefits and improving workplace safety. Union membership peaked in the early 1970s and has since been in steady decline. Some individuals in union leadership positions are very reasonable, fair and enjoyable to work with. They do their best to protect the rights of their workers and negotiate for increased pay and benefits. Others, unfortunately, don't look at the big picture and constantly create friction by making totally unreasonable demands.

The companies where I worked figured out that if you don't take care of your people, the unions will. Another common saying was that you will get the union that you deserve. We preferred non-union operations over union representation because it allowed for more flexibility. We kept our salaried operations pay and benefits better than the union sites yielding no good reason a site would vote for union representation unless the site had poor leadership. I'm proud to say that I've never had a site vote to be represented by a union.

As I said earlier, the people you work with make the difference. I've worked with some union leaders that do everything they can to protect workers, even those that blatantly break the rules and are very poor performers. On the other hand, some union leaders are primarily concerned with fairness for their workers and don't hesitate to address problem performers directly.

One example was when I became plant superintendent for the Epichlorohydrin production unit at Dow. Epichlorohydrin is a chemical intermediate used in downstream products such as food products, epoxy resins and plastics. One advantage (and disadvantage) of unions is the company-union contract that details specific agreements and rules agreed to by the union and the company.

One of those agreements was that overtime should be distributed fairly, but the individual units could determine how to accomplish the distribution. The Epichlorohydrin plant had a fair system for distributing overtime. If you were offered and turned down an overtime shift, the turn down would count the same as if you had accepted it. In addition, a clause provided that if you had vacation scheduled the day before or after one of your long weekends, you would not be charged for overtime you turned down during that long weekend.

One of the operators, Dan, was gaming the system and upsetting his co-workers. Dan's behavior had become a huge issue in the unit. At the beginning of each year, Dan scheduled a day of vacation adjacent to each of his long weekends. As the year progressed, he would cancel his vacation the day before it was scheduled, after overtime for the weekend had been offered. He had "gamed the system" so that he had his long weekend off and wasn't charged for any overtime offered. Naturally, Dan's actions made the other operators furious. When I arrived and heard about the problem, I read the union contract carefully and saw that another agreement stated supervision had the option to approve or not approve vacation that was scheduled or canceled, which almost never happened. To address the situation, I told Dan I would not approve any more of his vacation cancellations.

Of course, Dan was upset and called the union boss who went by the name of "the Duke." The Duke was a tough guy and had a huge reputation across the site. The other operators and I listened as Dan talked to the Duke on the telephone and told him how unfair I was being. Dan then handed the telephone to me and said, "The Duke wants to talk to you." The Duke told me, "Sam, this doesn't sound like you, you aren't being very fair. Sometimes people change their plans and you should allow them to cancel their vacation if they want to."

I then explained to the Duke that Dan had not told him the entire story and explained what Dan was *actually* doing. After hearing it, the Duke agreed with me and said I was doing the right thing. I hung up the telephone and Dan asked with a smirk on his face, "What did the Duke say?" I answered, "The Duke said I can do whatever I want," and walked away. We never had another problem with Dan and the overtime system again. I also gained a lot of respect from the other operators.

The point is to be as fair as you can with your people, but also to address problem performers head on. The Duke was a tough guy, but also very reasonable which I appreciated. Another lesson, if you work in a Union represented facility, read every line of the contract. The contracts are written to protect both parties.

Dealing with problem performers can be almost the same in a union or non-union environment if you do it the right way. The main principles are to treat people fairly and to address problems openly with the individual. If you take measurable actions to improve performance, most of the time the employee will improve. It's critical to document every step of the way. By following this process, I never had a problem terminating an individual that didn't respond and improve, both in union and non-union operations.

Works councils in Europe are required by law in many countries. The works council consists of employees voted into the council by their peers. The primary cause of major problems with works councils is when company management decides major change is needed, such as organization change or downsizing the organization, and plans it all out before consulting the works council. They surprise the works council, which immediately sets up conflict and a bad confrontation.

The preferred method is to engage works councils early in the process. Explain to the works council the objectives and why they are important. "Tell" the council members what you need to accomplish and engage them on "how" best to accomplish it. This early collaboration provides a preferred starting point for the discussions and always leads to better results.

***GOAL ZERO NUGGET:***
*Address individual issues rather than punishing the entire team.*

# Contractors

Most companies utilize a fair number of contractors in their operations. It's just as important for contract employees to have the proper skills and competencies for their jobs as your employees. A contractor with the wrong skill set or work practice can cause significant problems.

OSHA only requires companies to report injuries and illnesses for their own employees. Contractor companies are responsible for reporting their own injuries and illnesses. When OSHA rules first came out, it was not uncommon to hear, "There was an injury in the plant, but it was just a contractor." The injury didn't count on the company's statistics. Most of us hated hearing this statement, and contractors were often treated as second class citizens.

Fortunately, the better companies began to record contractor injuries and illnesses the same as their own employees, providing a total worksite injury/illness rate. If your company isn't already reporting a total worksite injury/illness rate, I strongly encourage you to do so.

We made special efforts to treat all of our contractors with respect and eliminate any second-class citizen mentality. We worked hard to reduce the number of contractor companies we utilized and built strong partnerships. We did everything possible to indoctrinate their employees into our Goal ZERO culture from their first day on the job.

Legal considerations should be followed when working with contractors such as co-employer situations. Follow the legal guidelines, but still make the contractors feel like part of the team. Hire the right contractor companies; make sure their top management clearly understands your expectations; be firm, but fair, and always treat their employees with respect. Contractors are an important component for your success.

# People Metrics

As I have said so many times, you won't be able to accomplish anything without a highly skilled and motivated workforce.

Many factors change over time, both inside and outside of your company, that can impact your employees. For example, as I write this book, we are in the middle of the COVID-19 pandemic, which has drastically impacted the workplace environment.

To continually monitor your workforce and identify trends as they occur, you must identify the people metrics that are important to your organization. One of the best ways is to monitor compliance with your Operational Excellence Expectations Document. State your intentions as clearly as possible and then measure results regularly.

People metrics I've found to be helpful are:

- *Operational Excellence Expectations. Pick some of the critical expectations you have listed for people and track your progress.*
- *Employee turnover. A considerable amount of time and energy is spent hiring and developing the right employees. The loss is significant when a good employee leaves the company for another opportunity. Tracking the number of employees that leave, especially top performers, is essential. Track the exits by location and you'll be able to pinpoint issues early on.*
- *Absenteeism. Motivated people show up for work unless they are sick or have another significant reason. Absentee rates for individuals or departments can be an early warning signal of larger problems.*
- *Exiting employee survey data. It's a shame when you lose a good employee, but an essential action is to interview the person and find out why he/she left. Some people leave for reasons outside of your control, such as moving closer to family or getting an opportunity that you could not match. However, many leave due to their dissatisfaction, often due to their supervisor and management. It's important to find out whatever you can, track the data, and act.*
- *Diversity. A diverse workforce is powerful whether it is diversity of race, gender, or thought. Challenge your team to actively identify, hire, and develop high quality diverse candidates.*

- **Promotion rates.** Track the rate of promotion as a function of employee rating or performance evaluation. Make sure you are promoting the right people as appropriate.
- **Compensation.** Pay for performance has long been my mantra. Track the compensation level of your employees as a function of their performance level as well as their job size.
- **Experience level.** A sufficient level of experienced personnel is essential in a manufacturing plant managing hazardous materials. A healthy organization has a blend of experienced and new people, but never allows the experience level to fall too low.
- **Succession planning.** A mature organization has people who have the experience and skills ready to take on the next level job. Succession planning is important in any organization and you should track the health of your succession candidate list on a regular basis. Leaders should be held accountable for maintaining a healthy candidate pool within their organization.
- **Employee satisfaction.** Employee surveys are an important way to gain a broad understanding of your workforce opinions. Comments are especially useful. Integrate your Goal ZERO expectations into the survey questions. Break down the data by location or department. Averaging the data over a large company dilutes the real messages you are receiving.

# CHAPTER 5

## Safety—Protecting People and Saving Lives

The principles I have described in this entire book will help drive a paradigm shift in overall Operational Excellence performance in any organization. However, I couldn't write the book without offering a few leadership tips specifically on the subject of safety. Protecting people is vitally important. The best leaders know to lead with a strong emphasis on safety; it's the right thing to do, and it helps impact performance of everything else.

### The Five Causes of Safety Incidents— The Human Factor

Throughout the years, we analyzed many cases of injuries, incidents, and near misses. A very small percentage are caused by asset failure, but most fall into the people and system categories. By digging deeper, understanding the causes, and taking corrective actions, you are more able to proactively prevent incidents in the first place.

Our evaluation of the data has shown that most incident causes fall into five categories and not in any particular order:

1. *Leadership. Unclear expectations, inadequate skilled resources, ineffective monitoring, and lack of individual accountability and consequence management.*
2. *Competence. Individuals lack the basic skills and knowledge to do the job or task. Lack of understanding of requirements, procedures, and expectations.*
3. *Behavior. Carelessness, lack of attention to detail, mistakes, and lack of focus on the task. Failure to take time to recognize hazards. Lack of intervention for unsafe acts.*

4. ***Compliance.*** *Failure to follow rules and lack of a compliance culture. Ineffective self-assessments, auditing, timely corrective actions, and gap closure.*
5. ***Risk Management.*** *Inadequate identification of risks, improperly mitigating risks, and poor equipment maintenance.*

As you can see, all of these categories deal with human behavior. As we've mentioned several times, you must have a good management system, but competent people must execute the system to perfection to drive performance and achieve results.

Rather than experiencing a terrible incident with one of these five causes, it's better to *be proactive in each of these areas to prevent incidents.* Turn these root causes into action. Use these five causes as a checklist for your organization. Leadership is the key, as always. Make sure your people have the skills and competence to do their jobs and then hold them accountable. Identify and address system and individual performance issues quickly. Teach people to identify and mitigate risks. Develop a culture of attention to detail at all times to execute flawlessly and avoid mistakes. And finally, establish a 100% compliance, Goal ZERO culture.

# Personalize Safety

I have a very good friend from Dow, Alex Pollock, who is one of the most enthusiastic and positive individuals I have ever met. Alex refers to certain individuals as being in his mental health club. He has many sayings, but one that always stuck in my mind was, "People don't care what you know, they want to know that you care."

This quote is so true, especially when you are dealing with the topic of safety. It's so easy to become obsessed with metrics such as OSHA recordable rates and lost time incidents. However, safety is not about the numbers, it's about protecting people. More important, it's about preventing the terrible consequences that friends and family must suffer when a loved one gets seriously injured.

In our Goal ZERO workshops, we spent a lot of time asking our people to think about the personal aspects of an injury; not only the consequences for themselves, but also for their friends and family. We talked about the life events you might miss such as watching your children grow, playing sports with them, watching dance lessons, or attending their wedding. Many of our people told us how these sessions changed their lives and their behavior—and how much they believed in the importance of Goal ZERO.

Intervention when witnessing an unsafe act with others is a powerful tool in the workplace. We emphasized being your brother's keeper and watching out for each other. We all get in a hurry and take shortcuts at times. We found that most people are not comfortable intervening with others. Therefore, we provided tips and guidance on how to conduct interventions in a positive way.

Intervention during an unsafe act doesn't take much time and can be a rewarding experience. Telling a person "why" you are intervening has a powerful effect. It's actually easy. For example, if Susan is working at heights and isn't properly tied off, you can say, "Susan, I see you aren't properly tied off. I care about you and would hate to see you fall and suffer a serious injury. An injury would have a serious impact on your family. How about buckling up?" Susan will normally reply, "Thanks, I really appreciate your intervention. I was in a hurry and forgot to tie off." Susan ties off and you have actually improved your relationship because she knows you care.

As the leader, I often told my co-workers, "If you see me doing something unsafe such as hustling down the hall too fast for a meeting, please intervene and ask me to slow down. That intervention might help me avoid a slip and fall, and possibly an injury, from spilled coffee on the floor." We all need to watch out for each other.

One of our most popular programs was putting pictures of family members, friends, or pets on the back of the identification badges people wore. Along with the picture, it said, "This is why I work safe." We would blow the pictures up poster size and place them along the walls of our buildings. These posters were immensely popular during large "maintenance turnarounds" of our manufacturing facilities in which we brought in hundreds

132 The Power of Goal ZERO

of contractors. The pictures of loved ones served as a constant safety reminder to each of them.

Any time a significant incident occurs, it's crucial for leadership to go to the site as soon as possible. The first purpose is to show care for the people who will be understandably shaken. Comfort and reassurance during times like these are extremely important. The other reason for going to the scene quickly is to learn and see the situation for yourself. It's amazing how much you can learn immediately following an incident while everything is fresh on people's minds.

# Behavior—Task Specific

An essential factor in good safety performance is an individual's personal behavior on each and every task. Many routine tasks that individuals typically perform are considered to be low risk. However, mistakes in these types of tasks can often lead to personal injury, operational impact, quality incidents or negative customer consequences.

How many times have you noticed that a person may be acting differently today than he or she did yesterday or last week? Many factors can affect the human brain. A person may have had a bad night's sleep, he might be getting sick, or she might have a major family issue taking place. And of course, people may be influenced by drugs or alcohol. It's important to know the people on your team and be aware of subtle changes in their behavior.

The expectation of a Goal ZERO culture is for individuals to perform every task with zero defects. Working with zero defects is much easier said than done. No one is perfect and people make mistakes, but you can implement programs and practices that significantly reduce the risk of error.

Football is an excellent example. The top coaches understand they have the best chance of winning if every play is executed to perfection, one play at a time. For each play, every player needs to concentrate on the signal count so he doesn't jump offsides. Then he needs to perform his individual assignment to perfection. If each player on the team executes well, the play has a good chance of being successful.

Business is the same. You want each of your employees to perform each task to perfection, one task at a time. Carpenters understand this concept very well and you'll hear them say, "Measure twice, cut once." Work hard to develop a culture of excellence in performance.

Daydreaming is something we all do. How many times have you gone into another room to get something and when you get there, you forget what you went to get? Have you ever been getting dressed in the morning and forget whether you brushed your teeth or not? Doing one thing while thinking about something else can lead to mistakes that can have significant consequences, especially in the workplace.

Throughout the years, I've come across many themes and programs designed to keep people focused on the task at hand. Here are a few examples:

- *Pre-task analysis. Many companies utilize this analysis, which requires the employee or work group to think through the job and make sure they understand the risks, are taking the right precautions, have the right tools, and can do the job safely. A pre-prepared checklist is often utilized. A downside to a checklist is it can become so routine that employees begin to "check the box" without giving it the thought that is needed. Therefore, keep it fresh and rotate processes from time to time.*
- *Check Signals. This mental process requires every employee to answer three questions before each task:*
    *1) What can go wrong?*
    *2) What precautions do I need to take?*
    *3) Can I do the job safely?*
- *Eyes on Path. People should use this simple technique when moving from one location to another to avoid tripping hazards.*
- *Look up, look down, look all around. This practice helps employees identify potential hazards by becoming more aware of the surroundings in their workplace.*
- *Do what you are doing. This one simply reminds people to concentrate on the job they are doing at the time. If you find yourself thinking about something else, stop! Take*

*some time to process your other thoughts and then get back to the task at hand.*

- *Focus—Start to Finish. This mantra helps to reinforce with individuals the need to focus on what they are doing, from start to finish when doing a task. Avoid distractions that can lead to mistakes and defects.*
- *Intervention. This technique allows individuals to feel free to give or receive an intervention if someone is performing an unsafe act or is not concentrating on the task at hand. We all need to help each other.*

All these approaches help drive incident-free performance. Keep your approach fresh since everyone can become complacent over time. Use frequent examples of bad incidents and results as reminders of consequences that can occur by inattention to detail. These techniques and many others are various ways to help and remind people to keep their mind on what they are doing. Inattention to detail is one of the leading causes of incidents.

# Avoiding Unsafe Acts

Mother Nature is actually quite forgiving. If someone drops an object from heights, the chance that you will be hit is quite low since the space surrounding you is much larger than your body. Odds are good that you will not be in the wrong place at the wrong time.

Flammable materials typically have narrow flammability ranges. If the fuel/oxygen ratio is too high or too low, the material won't ignite. I can remember times when we had accidental hydrocarbon releases that didn't ignite, for which I was always extremely thankful.

Therefore, the chances of a near miss are much greater than an injury. The difference between a near miss, a minor incident, and a fatality is often based on luck. I don't know about you, but I don't want to rely on luck to remain safe. Be sure to investigate high potential near misses the same as you would if a tragic result occurred.

In a Goal ZERO culture, we rely on personal behaviors, not luck, to assure our safety. Avoiding unsafe acts is one of the basic and easiest behaviors of Goal ZERO. Eliminating unsafe acts is one of the best ways to reduce your chance of injury.

Here's a simple example to illustrate my point. If I stand on a chair or table to reach a light fixture, I have already performed an unsafe act. Chances are, I will probably finish the task without incident. However, there's a chance I might fall off of the table. If I fall, I might get lucky and not get hurt. However, I might get bruised, break an arm, or even receive a head injury and die.

The point is, I should have done the job safely in the first place by taking the time to get a ladder instead of standing on the chair or the table. The concept is simple; ZERO unsafe acts by all people at all times, even for small jobs. Watch out for each other and intervene as needed.

Avoiding unsafe acts and unnecessary risks is important on and off the job. Injury rates are much, much higher off the job than they are at work. We instilled in our people to live the Goal ZERO culture at home like they do at work. Discuss the concept with your friends and family. Take the extra time to conduct home activities safely, such as working with electricity, making a repair at heights, using knives, or lifting heavy objects. Remembering Goal ZERO might make the difference in helping a friend or family member prevent a very serious injury. We often said, "We want you to go home safely each day and we also want you to return to work the same way."

# Alarm Management

I learned about the importance of alarm management in process control systems during my first manufacturing assignment at the Allyl Chloride unit. Allyl Chloride is a chemical intermediate used in the production of pharmaceuticals, plastics, pesticides, epoxy glue, and numerous food products. When I arrived, the alarm panel in the control room had about 120 active alarms while the plant was actually running normally.

To say the least, the discipline of alarm management in the unit was atrocious. The third week that I was working in the plant, a tank of highly flammable allyl chloride overflowed and filled the surrounding dike area. The high-level alarm wasn't working and had been active for weeks. Fortunately, the material never ignited, and the spill was cleaned up, but I never forgot the incident and the importance of alarm management.

Alarm management became a high priority for me, and the lessons remained throughout my career. Alarm management takes diligence and special attention at all times. I surely hope that no plant exists today with that dismal level of active alarms.

In a Goal ZERO environment, the objective is to operate your plant with zero active alarms. Everyone plays a role in achieving this objective. The operator needs to take action on any alarm that becomes active. The instrument technicians need to keep the instruments working. The engineers and programmers need to eliminate nuisance alarms, making sure that every alarm is important and requires action.

And finally, measurements are important. A few key metrics to use regularly are:

- *Number of active alarms at any given time*
- *Alarms that have been active for more than 24 hours*
- *Frequency of individual alarms*
- *Alarm overload (number of alarms that activate during a process upset)*

The last one is important during times of plant upsets. It's easy for programmers to add all types of alarms, but you don't want an operator to get overloaded with alarms during times of trouble. Plant operational upsets are critical times and important alarms can be overlooked if the alarm flooding is too severe. Numerous industry alarm management standards and recommended practices are available to help with this important work.

When you enter a control room, the number of active alarms is a good, quick indicator of how well the plant is operated and maintained. In a Goal ZERO plant, operators take pride when they keep their alarm panel clear of alarms. It takes discipline and diligence and is worthy of recognition and appreciation to the operators when they are doing well.

# Keeping Safety Awareness High

As you progress towards becoming a Goal ZERO company, injuries and incidents will be much less frequent. In fact, smaller departments and locations should not have an injury for many years. A Goal ZERO workplace is terrific, but the side effect is that people can become complacent and drop their guard.

Through the years, I saw many times how a particular location reacted following a serious injury. People in the organization developed an intense focus, conducted all types of safety discussions, and started emphasizing the basics. The sense of urgency was high. Everyone was extremely careful not to have an incident and get hurt. If you've ever been in an automobile accident, you know the feeling. For a long time thereafter, your level of attention is at an all-time high when driving and it's quite a while before you become relaxed in a car again.

We recognized the need to help those injury free locations keep their safety awareness high at all times. One of the best techniques was the "Safety Flash." This one-page email blast went to everyone in the company immediately following an injury, incident, or any significant event elsewhere in the company. It was critical that the communication went out quickly to have the maximum effect.

A Safety Flash typically had a flashy, attention grabbing header. The Safety Flash contained a photo of the incident or something similar. It only stated the facts that were known at the time. Since investigations had not yet been performed, we didn't speculate on the causes or corrective actions. The intention was to show a sense of urgency and the importance to the organization. For significant incidents, the results of the investigation were sent out later as a follow-up.

At each location, supervision printed copies to post on bulletin boards and place at various places such as lunch tables. If appropriate, the incident was discussed during various meetings. These flashes always created considerable discussion and helped to keep safety and attention to detail on the minds of our people. The main theme was always, "Let's act like this incident just happened here. What actions would we be taking if the incident had occurred in our workplace?"

Another useful tool was a "Safety Alert." A safety alert was typically sent for incidents that occurred outside of our company. We believed that no incident should go to waste; every incident should be used as a learning and improvement opportunity. We sent Safety Alerts to the organization to remind people of the items in our management system that would have prevented the same type of incidents. They served as a periodic reminder of why our requirements and processes were so important.

> **GOAL ZERO NUGGET:**
> *Be proactive to prevent complacency.*

# Global Safety Day

I was always searching for new ways to get people's attention and improve safety performance. One extremely helpful concept we developed was conducting a Global Safety Day each year. We perfected this program through the years and conducted it annually the last 11 years of my career.

The purpose of Safety Day was to dedicate one day each year for the entire global organization to discuss and focus on safety, and what it meant to work in a Goal ZERO company. The concept was primarily focused on individual behavior since behavior is such an important factor in achieving safe performance. Over time, the topics expanded to health, security, environmental protection, and other pertinent areas, but we kept the name consistent, so people always knew what to expect. We wanted to conduct a day so powerful and impactful that every participant would leave work at the end of the day with a renewed sense of dedication to working in a Goal ZERO manner. Safety Day provided a terrific venue for establishing a Goal ZERO culture of excellence.

We began each year by selecting a theme, which always had an element of behavior and action embedded in it. Some of the Global Safety Day themes were Goal ZERO Begins with

Me, Goal ZERO—Focus Start to Finish, Goal ZERO—100%, and Performing at Our Best Every Day.

We then selected a global steering team and site steering teams. We provided some high-level concepts and guidelines, but the power was in the teams thinking about and developing their own individual programs and what they needed to accomplish. By maximizing the number of people involved in the planning, we were well on our way to an effective program.

The locations designed their Global Safety Day around maximum active employee participation, not just listening to presentations. The most effective activities involved small group discussion sessions in which someone introduced a particular subject and then facilitated open discussions. Discussion topics included the impact on your family and friends if you were seriously injured, how you can intervene if someone is performing an unsafe act, telling others why it's okay to intervene with you, areas where we could improve in our department, and the importance of always following rules.

No other meetings were to be conducted on Global Safety Day which allowed leadership's full participation in the day's events. Executive Team members were assigned different locations to attend and participate. Following the first Global Safety Day we conducted at Shell, our CEO, Jeroen van der Veer, told me Safety Day was the first event he had seen that captured the attention and participation of the entire global organization so well.

Needless to say, Global Safety Day was a huge success each year and it provided the right setting for communicating Goal ZERO expectations and also listening to our employees. Our employees told us they were proud to work for a company that cared so much for their safety.

---

# CHAPTER 6

---

## Management System
## Concepts that Work

*"It's a funny thing about life; if you refuse to accept anything but the best, you very often get it." –* **W. Somerset Maugham**

World-class organizations and results driven leaders seek to reduce variation, drive for consistency, and fine tune the way work gets done. Build on the best practices that work and expect excellence in every detail. Knowledge and key information should be anchored in a management system. It makes no sense for people to continually "reinvent the wheel." A good management system along with a Goal ZERO culture creates discipline that leads to improved performance in any organization.

It's important to align on the concept of a management system. Some consider a management system as an operating model. My simple definition is that it is an organized, disciplined structure for documenting "how we do things around here." A management system should be clear to understand and serve as a useful reference for people in the organization.

When you have a good functioning management system, your people will look back and wonder how they ever functioned without it. The concept is a good example of common sense. Ralph Waldo Emerson once wrote, "Society is always taken by surprise at any new example of common sense."

Good management systems contain many elements, but some of the most important ones are expectations for the organization, clear accountability for each of the expectations, required standards, technology and acquired knowledge, work processes that assure effectiveness and efficiency, measurements, performance reporting, governance, and a regular cadence for overall management. Standardized ways of doing work drive efficiency, effectiveness, quality, alignment, and add discipline to the organization. By standardizing the basic work, people are free to be more creative and move faster on their other areas of focus.

How would you describe the perfect management system? A few of the key words that come to my mind are simplicity, crisp, intuitive, logical, fit for purpose, helpful, user-friendly, and up to date. Start with the end in mind and develop your system to fit the user's needs.

In this chapter, I'll describe various work processes and methods we found to be helpful in building a world-class management system. I'll share many tips to assure the elements of the management system are effective and meet the needs of the organization. In addition, I'll highlight some of the work processes that are particularly useful at improving performance such as self-assessments, auditing, investigations, the "why" review, learning from experience and high potential incidents.

A good management system is so important for any organization, but why do so many get it wrong? It's no one's fault; documents are typically written by many different authors through the years with a lack of consistent format or style. The result is a system that has morphed over time without an overall structure or organization of documentation.

Many companies experience a series of problems or a major incident and you'll hear leadership say, "We need to get back to the basics." I've heard this phrase many times through the years and I'll bet you have too. Why do we have to keep learning this same lesson over and over? You can be proactive by creating an effective management system that becomes the cornerstone of your company's operating culture. Once you have an effective system and execute with a Goal ZERO mentality, you'll never have to "get back to the basics" again.

The key to the success of your management system is to create documents that people in the organization want to use rather than are forced to use. Users want to know why the documents are important, see the value, find information they need quickly and then get back to work. The management system becomes an enabling tool that is helpful to them. Make the system and sub processes intuitive. People shouldn't need any special training if you develop your documents by working back from what the user actually needs. Your employees will trust the system if the tools, processes, and information help them to work smarter.

Finally, the next worst thing to not having a management system is having one that's not maintained and is out of date. Unfortunately, this scenario if very common in many organizations due to no one being assigned to maintain the system and the lack of a process for capturing and organizing learnings. Your management system will be continually updated if you follow the guidance in this book.

> **GOAL ZERO NUGGET:**
> *A management system documents best practices*
> *and enables focus on achieving excellence.*

# Prioritize, Standardize, and Clarify

Progressing through each company in my career, I increasingly understood the power of standardization and simplicity. We worked to reduce our number of requirements, improved clarity of each requirement and increased the focus on full compliance. To provide some examples, and perhaps some similar to your current situation, I'll describe a few of my experiences.

At my summer job with Exxon in 1974, I was working at the huge Gas Processing Plant near Kingsville, Texas. Exxon had a series of company-wide operating manuals for Gas Processing. The manuals were written in a practical manner and easy to understand. Every gas plant in Exxon relied on the knowledge and information in these manuals.

ExxonMobil was an early leader in the use of standardized management systems. Its system is called the Operational Excellence Management System, OEMS, and is well known across the industry. I'm confident that OEMS is one of the primary enablers of ExxonMobil's long-term operational success.

At Dow Chemical, the company had a long history of a good management system. It was called the Operating Discipline Management System, ODMS. In addition, we had a concept of global expertise centers consisting of subject matter experts accountable for the rules and processes in their particular area. These expertise centers were charged with collecting and communicating best practices across the organization and were extremely effective.

When I became Vice President of EH&S at Dow, I began to understand how some of our onerous global standards and requirements made compliance difficult and, in fact, created problems. We soon began work to improve the clarity and understanding of the requirements in our management system.

When I arrived at Shell in 2004, I found that the company governance structure was quite different. Royal Dutch Shell was a joint venture with numerous subsidiaries and the organization was managed by a "Committee of Managing Directors." The legal guidance was that the parent organization could not dictate requirements for the "independent" operating subsidiaries. Each of the operating companies had full autonomy—quite the opposite from my experience at Exxon and Dow.

The lack of a standardized approach and consistency across the organization resulted in significant problems. In 2003, a year before I joined Shell, the company had experienced a major setback when the Securities and Exchange Commission (SEC) found that the company had been accounting for oil and gas reserves differently in various countries. Shell had to significantly restate its reserves, resulting in a 20% reduction, the company stock taking a major hit, and the termination of the Chairman of the Committee of Managing Directors and Executive Vice President of Upstream. There was significant value destruction.

The SEC determined that Shell could no longer operate with such global inconsistency and non-compliance with the rules. As a result, Shell began to hire global functional leaders, such as myself, to improve global functions and drive consistency globally. In 2005, the joint venture was abolished, and Royal Dutch Shell became one company with a single CEO for the entire organization. The result was a green light for global consistency, and we wasted no time moving forward and driving standardization across the company.

One of the first examples was with motor vehicle accidents, which had been a major cause of injuries and incidents. Motor vehicles included trucks delivering products as well as individual vehicles. We had 20,000 trucks on the road daily delivering gasoline, jet fuel and other products. Everything at Shell was huge. I commissioned a small team to develop a safe driving standard. The first draft the team presented to me was 67 pages. However, I wanted a much shorter document, one that every driver could read and remember.

I sent the team back to tighten up the document. One of the team members said, "Sam, I think I've got it. You want the 10 Commandments, not the Bible!" I chuckled and said, "That's right, you have it." The final document was only a handful of pages. It was a simple document containing only the most important requirements that every driver could easily understand and follow. This new safe driving standard was the beginning of our simplification process for requirements at Shell.

By the time I was recruited to LyondellBasell in 2009, I had reached full stride in my approach to Operational Excellence. LyondellBasell had been created in early 2008 when Basell (a private Dutch company) purchased Lyondell (a publicly traded US company). This transaction occurred just prior to the economic crisis of 2008 and the merger quickly failed. The company declared bankruptcy in early 2009. The two companies had never fully integrated and very little consistency in the management system and associated processes existed.

Legacy Lyondell had a complex set of overbearing documents with many requirements. Legacy Basell had a handful of optional guidelines. The performance results were not up to expectations. A significant process safety incident was occurring every other week in which the primary cause was either non-compliance or not following a well-known standard in another part of the company.

I knew that to truly achieve progress in overall performance, it would take a concerted multi-functional approach to simplify the system, develop standards, implement work processes, eliminate variation, and drive performance improvement. In addition, by driving a Goal ZERO culture leading with safety, I knew we would achieve benefits in reliability, quality, cost control, and many other areas.

One of my first actions was to form an Operational Excellence Leadership Team (OELT) consisting of the heads of Manufacturing, Human Resources, Legal, Business, and myself. I led the team and we had the full and complete support from the CEO. We wanted to break down the barriers between functions, making sure we had agreement at the highest level for any new standards, rules, and processes we developed. Human resources representation was critical at the table since so much of our success was based on the performance of our people. Business representation on the team was vital because a cost was often associated with any new requirement and it was important to have their support from the very beginning. As a member of the OELT, I personally reviewed and edited every line of every revised standard to make sure it was fit for purpose. I used my years of plant management experience and always asked the question, "Would I be comfortable with this requirement if I were a plant manager?"

As we began to develop our management system, we first created a list of Operational Excellence Expectations to guide the organization. Then we developed an entirely new set of global standards, initiated new work processes, and began to empower the various functional groups. We created a system in which the mandatory requirements were succinct and easy to understand.

All of this effort led to the creation of our management system, which we called Technology and Knowledge Management (TKM). We created a series of Excellence Models for each major category of work. The Excellence Models contained the priority information associated with each topic: technology, mandatory standards, procedures, best practices, work processes, training information, and reference material. Once we established a good Operational Excellence Management System, we were able to primarily focus on flawless execution driving rapid transformation of performance improvement.

# Management Systems

A management system is a collection of information that includes knowledge, requirements, and work processes. The system describes how work is conducted. Simplicity is important. People love working in an organization that has a good, fit for purpose management system. A good system provides clarity, captures learnings and best practices, improves efficiency, adds discipline, and enables accelerated progress.

In many cases, an organization's so-called management system has become too complex over the years and provides a false sense of security. In other cases, documents exist but never get used. Leaders will claim they have a management system, but how well is it followed in the organization? Can people find the information they need? Is there consistency across the organization?

Most organizations need to update their management system and improve the way information is organized. A few of the problems that organizations have with their management systems are:

- *It's not easy for people to find the information they need in an efficient manner.*
- *Too many complex documents have been developed over the years.*
- *New documents continue to be created, but nothing ever seems to be deleted.*
- *Information is not organized in a consistent manner.*
- *Confusion with requirement interpretation exists in the organization.*
- *It's difficult to institutionalize learnings from incidents to prevent recurrence.*
- *High priority items are mixed with low priority information.*
- *Too much knowledge resides in people's heads and is not captured for the organization.*
- *Repeat incidents occur because organizations fail to learn and remember from the past.*
- *No one is in charge of information management.*

These issues have been apparent in almost every company I've dealt with. The advent of computers has proliferated the problem. It becomes easier for people to generate numerous documents and more difficult for users to find the most important information they need.

These problems can be prevented by applying proactive management to information overload. A management system has two primary stakeholder groups: subject matter experts for each topic and the users in the organization who are expected to comply with the system.

The subject matter experts want tools for how and where to store their information and documentation. They also want to make it easier for new subject matter experts to get up to speed quickly and build on what has already been developed rather than working on the same old issues or drastically changing direction.

The users in the field want "simplicity." They want to be able to find the right information they need in an efficient manner. The users don't want to sift through considerable amounts of information to determine what is most important. They believe that the subject matter experts should prioritize the information for them. Operations people often say, "Just tell me what I have to do, and I'll do it."

Meeting the needs of both stakeholders isn't difficult. Begin by developing guidance and expectations for your management system. A few examples of guidance for the system to ensure alignment of subject matter experts and users in the field are:

1. *Easy to find information*
2. *Consistent design and structure*
3. *Prioritization of important information*
4. *Very clear listing of mandatory requirements*
5. *Examples of good practices*
6. *Past incidents and learnings*
7. *Training materials*
8. *Access to subject matter experts*
9. *User friendly software*

Once an updated company-wide system is in place, local sites and departments can build on the framework and add additional details for how they operate locally. The result for the end user is a local system with items such as procedures and local rules that build on the succinct corporate management system. The system should be fit for purpose.

Consistent terminology and vocabulary are critical to avoid confusion in the organization, especially if you conduct business in countries with different native languages. Providing clarity and ease of understanding are important to the organization. A good functioning management system provides a consistent platform for which leaders can lead.

Management systems can be organized in a variety of manners. The easiest way is to group items into "Management System Categories" that make sense for your organization. Each category can have several sub processes. An "Excellence Model" is then created for each sub process.

Here is an example for a petrochemical company:

### Management System Categories
### (Petrochemical Industry Example)

1. ***Technology***
   *This section documents the technology for "how" to produce your particular product or provide your service. Excellence models might include:*
   a. *Refining*
   b. *Polyethylene*
   c. *Epoxy*
   d. *Glycerine*

2. ***Operations and Support***
   *This section of the management system includes standards and operating practices that are common across all of your various process technologies. Excellence Models include:*
   a. *Common operating practices*
   b. *Maintenance*
   c. *Reliability*
   d. *Turnarounds*
   e. *Capital projects*
   f. *Energy*
   g. *Utilities*

3. ***Asset Integrity***
   *The Asset Integrity section includes standards, processes, and procedures for design, maintenance, inspection, and operation of your equipment and facilities. Excellence Models include:*
   a. *Stationary Equipment*
   b. *Machinery*
   c. *Instruments and analyzers*

    d. *Electrical*
    e. *Utilities*
    f. *Engineering Standards*

4. **Health, Safety, Environment, and Security**
   *Functional activities are included in this section.*
   *Excellence Models include:*
    a. *Personal Safety*
    b. *Process Safety*
    c. *Product Safety*
    d. *Environmental*
    e. *Industrial Hygiene*
    f. *Medical*
    g. *Security*

5. **Human Resources**
   *The management system is the perfect place to document work processes for the human resources function. The people component for achieving Operational Excellence is essential and full alignment is key. Example topics include recruiting, hiring, onboarding, training, talent development, succession planning, leadership assessment, and development.*

6. **Include additional support functions such as Procurement, Supply Chain, etc., as appropriate.**

> **GOAL ZERO NUGGET:**
> *Management systems enable discipline.*

# Excellence Models

An Excellence Model is developed for each sub process of the global category. The Excellence Model includes all documentation, information, and collective knowledge for the subprocess. The Excellence Models are organized in a consistent manner for ease of access and utilization. Each Excellence

Model looks and feels the same so people in the organization become comfortable and competent at using the system and finding information.

Establish a Tier 1, Tier 2, and Tier 3 framework for organizing material in each Excellence Model. Include a section in each Excellence Model listing people with appropriate levels of expertise. A typical Excellence Model will have these sections:

### Tier 1 (Mandatory requirements)
- *Critical few documents*
- *Standards, policies, procedures, and mandatory processes*
- *Fully auditable*

### Tier 2 (Preferred practices)
- *Limited and controlled number of documents*
- *Highly encouraged work practices and processes*
- *Locations have flexibility to deviate if they can meet the intent in other ways*

### Tier 3 (Guidance and reference material)
- *Past incidents and learnings*
- *Educational material*
- *Tools, templates, lessons learned*
- *Reference material*
- *Internal and external information*
- *Metrics and Key Performance Indicators*

### Excellence Model Resources
- *Excellence Model owners*
- *Excellence Model teams*
- *Extended networks*
- *Individuals with expertise*

Excellence Models contain the information necessary to establish consistency across the organization. Local sites and departments follow the same format for their site-specific Tier 1, 2, and 3 documents. Detailed procedures, local rules, and processes are included in the site-specific section of the Excellence Models. A good Operational Excellence software system provides a digitized structure for aligning corporate and local information in an easy-to-use format. The software capitalizes on the latest technology to digitize the execution of your system and capture maximum value.

It's amazing how much a consistent framework and way of working can help the effectiveness of an organization. Once the Excellence Model framework is established, work becomes much more efficient. For the first time, document generators know how and where to store their documents. And more importantly, users know how to find and use them.

A clear owner must be assigned for each Excellence Model, such as a Process Safety Excellence Model Owner. In a large company, the owner can be assisted by an Excellence Model Team. The individuals on the team must be active and have very clear role responsibilities that include prioritizing, writing, maintaining, and updating the information in the Excellence Model.

The Excellence Model Owner and team sort through all existing documentation, prioritize information, simplify each document, and insert the prioritized documents into the new Excellence Model framework. The benefit is that you can begin utilizing the concept rather quickly. You always have more available documents than you need, and many are too complex. Strict prioritization is essential.

# Excellence Model Roles and Responsibilities— The People Element

Clear expectations for Excellence Model Owners and teams will determine how they approach their job and the work product they deliver. They will do a better job of prioritizing requirements if they know a process for multi-functional approval will take place.

Assigning individual responsibilities and accountabilities for Excellence Model Owners and teams is another example of the Divide and Conquer approach. Each person has a role description to make sure expectations are clear and to eliminate confusion. The following list includes some important roles for a large company. For smaller organizations the teams and networks may not be necessary. In almost all cases, these roles are part-time. Use caution to not create additional full-time functional overhead.

- *Excellence Model Owner. This individual has the sole ownership of the Excellence Model. If more than one person owns it, nobody owns it.*
- *Excellence Model Team. Each Excellence Model has a team to work with the owner to develop and maintain the Excellence Model. The members of the Team are expected to "do work and contribute," not just attend meetings. Each person has specific assignments.*
- *Excellence Model Extended Network. This group of interested individuals for the topic is used for two-way communication and collaboration.*
- *Site Excellence Model Focal Point. This individual at each site is responsible and accountable for transferring the Excellence Model information to the site. These individuals functionally report to the Operational Excellence Leader at the particular site.*

It's important to assign an overall coordinator for the Operational Excellence Management System for the company. Every Excellence Model should be created with the same methodology and format. The coordinator is critical to keep progress moving in a consistent manner. Coaching the Excellence Model Owners and their teams is important so they continue to deliver products consistently and meet desired expectations.

With the advent of the new Excellence Model System, we fundamentally changed the way our subject matter experts worked. They became much more proactive. Each Excellence Model Owner and Excellence Model Team had the accountability to develop and update their Excellence Model. Not only did the teams organize the documents into an Excellence Model, but they also began to update, simplify, and improve the documents. The owner and teams received and monitored company performance relative to their particular Excellence

Model. No longer were they only judged for what they knew, but also for how well they contributed to the Excellence Model and how well the organization performed in their area of focus.

By tracking the progress of each Excellence Model Team and with assigned due dates, technical organizations have a new sense of urgency for driving progress. Excellence Model Team agendas are proactively created to review and update the various documents in the Excellence Model. Each team member is expected to actively contribute and should be given a small percentage of time by his/her supervisor to work for the Excellence Model Team activities. Regularly review the performance of each team and change out members who don't contribute their fair share.

This structure provides career growth opportunities for technical professionals that should be integrated into your people management process. If you are a new person to the organization, the value proposition becomes clear. As you gain expertise in a particular area, you can be assigned to a Site Excellence Model Focal Point position, and in doing so, become a member of the Excellence Model Network. As you continue to grow, you can advance to become a member of the Excellence Model Team. Finally, you might even be chosen as the company Excellence Model Owner.

The Excellence Model Owners have considerable responsibility and should be given visible recognition. The position should become one that others aspire to achieve. Depending on the size of your organization and the number of Excellence Models, you might be able to assign a different person as the owner for each model. In all cases, create an expectation of ownership and delivery and not just knowledge of the particular subject. These responsibilities and expectations help raise the self-esteem of the professional community through their visible and proactive contributions to Operational Excellence. Every Excellence Model contributes to the overall success of the company.

# Consistency and Simplification

Some industry and company documents are problematic. Requirements are listed in standards and a few might be listed as "mandatory" requirements. What does that mean? If some requirements are mandatory, does it mean that others are not mandatory? In a Goal ZERO company, take out the word mandatory, otherwise people in your organization might think other requirements aren't mandatory. Goal ZERO means zero noncompliance with all requirements, it's the culture. Goal ZERO focuses on the positive aspects of expectations. People comply because they want to, not because they are forced to.

Complexity is a problem with the management systems in many companies. Documents have been created through the years by a wide variety of authors. The documents are too long and are not consistent. In addition, a common framework for the storage of information doesn't exist so it's difficult for users in the field to find the information they need.

Common terms in governance documents include shall, must, should, and may statements. Industry accepted definitions for these terms are:

- *"Shall" and "must" are mandatory items.*
- *"Should" indicates a recommended item.*
- *"May" is an optional item.*

In many documents, authors use these terms loosely and intermix them throughout standards. This inconsistency creates confusion and potential legal liability. Standards that include a combination of shall, should, and may statements confuse the user with items that are mandatory and those that are recommended.

With the advent of computers, standard writers have gotten into the terrible habit of installing multiple links within a document to other documents. These links lead to "standards within standards," which creates considerable confusion. It's easy for the author, but difficult for the reader. It doesn't make sense for the author of a standard to do what is easy for him/her, but make it confusing for years to come for the thousands of practitioners around the world that must use it.

The Excellence Model Owner and associated Excellence Model Team should drive clarity and simplicity. Simplification seems so obvious but is often missing within highly technical organizations. Three primary steps are important to accomplish simplification:

1. *Prioritize and minimize the number of documents in the Excellence Model.*
2. *Prioritize and minimize document content.*
3. *Simplify how each document is written.*

# Prioritize and Minimize Number of Documents

An Excellence Model consists of Tier 1, 2, and 3 documents. For any topic, an endless number of documents are available from many sources, both internal and external to the organization. Anyone can cram existing documents into these tiers and overload the system. Lack of prioritization is a huge mistake; it's easy but ineffective. Rigorous prioritization and simplification of documents are key to effective utilization and execution.

The responsibility of the Excellence Model Owner and the Excellence Model Team is to strictly prioritize and limit the number of documents that are included in Tiers 1, 2, and 3 of the Excellence Model. They should play a very strong gatekeeper role. Figure 5 is a graphical description for managing Tier 1, 2, and 3 information. Note that only the most important, value creating documents are included in the model. Think of the 80/20 model in which 20% of the information yields 80% of the results.

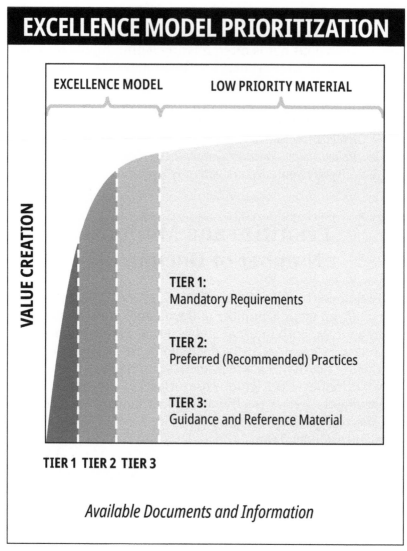

**FIGURE 5**
**Excellence Model Creation**

A corollary is conducting an internet search for information. When you conduct the search, you'll get a large number of results. However, you then must sort through the documents to determine the ones that are accurate, important, and relevant. Sorting the important from the less important is time consuming.

Utilizing Excellence Models should be different. The Excellence Model Owner and the Excellence Model Team should perform the prioritization work for the people in the organization. The owners and teams prioritize and then insert the documents into the appropriate Tier 1, 2, or 3 section of the Excellence Model based on their knowledge and experience. Their work has a multiplying effect on productivity, accuracy, and effectiveness.

# Prioritize and Minimize Document Content

In addition to minimizing the number of documents in your Excellence Model, it's important to minimize the length and amount of information in each of document, especially for Tier 1 documents. Some authors of documents ramble on, adding additional information with not much effort put into prioritization and document structure to help the reader. The authors believe that including everything possible is good, when it actually confuses the organization. The old quote applies perfectly, "I didn't have time to write you a short letter, so I wrote a long one instead."

When creating mandatory standards, success lies in prioritizing and including only the critical few items that are most important and that people can understand and remember. Culling out lower priority items is difficult to do, but extremely important. Too many requirements in standards makes it almost impossible for people to comply with all of them. Employees inherently begin to decide for themselves which elements of the standard are really important. Energy is spent on low priority items and the most critical requirements might end up with a low level of compliance. Lower priority items are better placed in Tier 2 preferred practice documents.

Shorter is always better and more effective. The challenge is getting everyone aligned on the same concepts. Provide a clear answer to the question, "What does good look like?" The authors and the users often have widely different concepts of a good and effective document.

- *Technical authors typically want to be complete and not omit anything. They do their research, gather all the data they can and believe it's all important.*
- *The users want documents to be short, clear, and concise. They don't want someone else to explain what is intended or to interpret the definition of a particular requirement.*

Figure 6 illustrates the point I am making when creating a Tier 1 corporate standard of mandatory requirements.

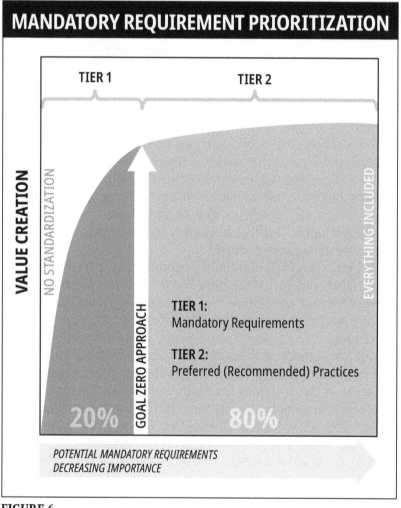

**FIGURE 6**
**Tier 1 Document Creation (Mandatory Requirements)**

Let's assume that this chart represents an individual Tier 1 company-wide standard containing mandatory requirements. One hundred potential requirements are available to include in the standard and they have been prioritized by importance from left to right.

With no corporate standardization at all (left-hand side of the chart) and every location developing its own set of requirements, the result is tremendous duplication of effort and considerable variation across the organization. On the other extreme, if the author includes all 100 potential requirements, which is commonly done in standards, the document becomes onerous to read and impossible to comply with, destroying value. The user spends valuable time complying with low priority items and is likely to miss compliance with one of the higher priority ones.

The secret for a Goal ZERO organization is to be very disciplined in limiting the number of mandatory requirements that make it into a Tier 1 document. The remaining, lower priority items can be included in an associated Tier 2 recommended practice document and allow flexibility at each location. Deliver a product the users want and will use, rather than everything the technical expert thinks is important.

The people in your organization are smart and trust is important. They can take the Tier 2 recommended practices and adopt them as requirements in their site management system or deviate depending on their particular situation. Once an item is written as a requirement, it must be complied with at all times—Goal ZERO performance.

In addition to prioritizing and minimizing the number of requirements in Tier 1 documents, be sure to only include "shall" statements as previously mentioned. All "should" statements, which imply recommended practice, should reside in Tier 2 support documents.

*GOAL ZERO NUGGET:*
*Reduce complexity through*
*disciplined prioritization.*

# Simplify the Documents

How many times have you tried to read a document and you find yourself underlining key points or even writing notes on a separate piece of paper just to understand what the document is trying to say? Don't let this confusion exist with your Excellence Model documents.

Subject matter experts will spend considerable time generating subject matter material and hopefully do a good job of prioritizing as I've explained. It makes sense to create documents that are easy to read and comprehend. Simplified systems begin with documents that are concise, clear, and easy to understand. The following sections provide recommendations for driving simplicity and tips for creating a simplified system.

# Simplicity

Simplicity is a prevailing theme throughout this book. Simplicity is the ability to make something easy to understand. Simplicity in a complex world is powerful. One of my favorite books is Simplicity by Bill Jensen. It's a must read. Bill Jensen looks at the human side of work focusing on what the organization needs. Many things are just too complex. He lays out an organized plan to cut through the mess or to completely eliminate it.

A few key points that are applicable to management systems and communication are:

- *Information should be user centered.*
- *By making the complex clear, it helps people to **work smarter**. It's a lot easier to figure out what's important and ignore what isn't.*
- *The way to reduce work complexity is to make it easier for the average employee to adapt the tools, processes, and information in the system to the way he or she needs to use them.*
- *Just because you have access to everything, doesn't mean you need it. People feel better about not having to see*

*everything. Being able to zoom in and out from the larger picture is important.*

- *Clutter stops you from breakthrough thinking. Anything that helps you organize your thinking is going to take you to a higher level.*
- *It's a lot easier to succeed when something is designed to help you get in, get what you need, and get out.*
- *Make it easier for people to find their own way and they'll be successful more often.*
- *Work backwards from what people need to work smarter. Most everyone is a lot smarter than we are letting them be.*

**GOAL ZERO NUGGET:**
*Making the complex seem simple is powerful.*

# Simplify Writing Style

Highly technical individuals often write in a style that may be difficult for others to understand. People are busy and don't have time to unpack overly long sentences and complex dictation. Documents should be written in the clearest and most understandable manner possible. Simplified writing is incredibly important but is often overlooked. To prevent complex writing, document writers should be trained and aligned on good writing practices.

Literary experts recommend that documents are most effective at the 8th grade reading level, where the average adult can easily read and comprehend the document. With a little training, document writers learn the factors that provide the best results:

- *Short and concise sentences*
- *Frequent use of bullet points*
- *Average amount of syllables per word*

It's not about dumbing down the content, but rather putting it in a format that people can understand. Ernest Hemingway was the king of short, concise sentences. He made every word count and kept his sentences simple and to the point.

Simplification of writing style is a terrific enabler for all documents in a management system. Train your document writers and hold them accountable. The hard, up front work of the subject matter experts on prioritization and simplification will yield time and efficiency savings across the organization for many years to come.

# Technical Writing— Flesch Reading Ease Score

An excellent tool for simplification of documents and readability is the utilization of the Flesch Reading Ease score and the Flesch-Kincaid Readability Test. Readability is the ease with which a reader can understand a written text. With this technique, document writers can be trained, and each document graded on readability.

Higher readability eases reading effort and speed for any reader, but it is especially important for those who do not have high reading comprehension. In readers with average or poor reading comprehension, raising the readability level of a text can make the difference between success and failure of your communication goals. Readability is especially true for documents such as procedures that are used by the broader population.

The scoring formula is based on the average number of words per sentence and the average syllables per word. The scoring criteria uses a scale from 0 to 100, with 0 being the most difficult and 100 the easiest to comprehend (higher score is better).

Tests have shown that Reader's Digest Magazine had a readability index of about 65, Time Magazine scored about 52, The Wall Street Journal about 43, The Harvard Law Review in the low 30s and a standard auto insurance policy of about 10.

Microsoft Word has the Flesch-Kincaid Readability Test

built into the software. After you complete a spell check, the Flesch Reading Ease score and the Flesch-Kincade Grade Level of the document are shown. We targeted our documents to be in the 60-70 Reading Ease score range. Other software programs offer similar methods for obtaining Reading Ease scores.

Setting clear expectations for document writers and then holding them accountable significantly improves readability and understandability. Creating easy to understand documents helps eliminate confusion, and the people on the front line greatly appreciate it.

**GOAL ZERO NUGGET:**
*Create documents with appropriate readability.*

# CHAPTER 7

## Work Processes for Achieving Operational Excellence

Progressing through the book, we have discussed leadership, people, management system and culture fundamentals for achieving Operational Excellence. The remainder of the book continues to build on the formula:

**Operational Excellence =
Leadership + People + Culture + Systems + Assets**

This chapter provides work processes that are particularly effective in good management system. Results driven leaders emphasize efficiency and consistency of the basic activities so that people have more time for creative and value generating actions. Many tools and processes are available to provide this consistency. A regular cadence of activities provides certainty and regularity for the organization. People know what to expect and the organization consistently improves. Remember that for every process, keep it simple and intuitive.

## Work Processes and Procedures

Practical work processes are important for a variety of reasons. A work process should be clear and understandable. If it's intuitive, you don't even realize you are following a work process. The way you organize your kitchen silverware, for example, is a simple process. Processes provide order, reduce variation, and improve efficiency when everyone understands and performs work in a consistent manner.

Process documents can often become much too complicated and, as a result, people don't follow them. Keep your work processes clear and practical. Strictly prioritize the steps that go into a work process, keep them at a high level, and don't try to micromanage every step. Procedures for critical activities are different and more detailed steps should be used for work in which every step is critical.

Detailed procedures are also an integral component of any management system. They should be continually improved and provide a consistent and safe manner for performing any task. Procedures are written in many different formats. The principles described in this book thus far all apply to procedures. Write them from the user point of view and use the Flesh Reading Ease method for clarity of understanding.

Procedures written in checklist format are most helpful to the front-line. People can follow the checklist as they are performing tasks and also write down recommended improvements for the procedure as they go. Follow the procedure or else change it. Keep procedures up to date, practical, intuitive, and people will follow them.

Don't bog down procedures with instructional material. Maintain instructional material and reference information in Tier 3 documents used for training and employee refreshment.

# Life-Critical Activities

My heart breaks every time I read or hear about a crane collapsing somewhere and people needlessly losing their lives. The technology and safe work practices exist to perform crane and rigging activities safely, and incidents should never occur.

This type of work falls into the category of life-critical activities. These are high risk activities which unfortunately have a long history of ending with catastrophic results if not performed correctly. These types of activities and associated incidents are well known. They have been investigated thoroughly each time and always end up with the same root causes falling into the leadership, people, culture, systems, and assets categories.

Its critical to identity the life-critical activities that are performed in your operations and the precautions that must be taken every time. Learn from the unfortunate experiences of others and never allow failure in these activities to occur.

A few examples of life-critical activities are:

- *Crane and Rigging*
- *Confined Space Entry*
- *Working at Heights*
- *Hot Work*
- *Initial Break into Equipment*

All standards and procedures must be followed in a Goal ZERO culture, but life-critical activities need an extra layer of detail, protection, and diligence. Communicate and review these requirements much more frequently. Any violation of requirements with a life-critical activity should be reported as a High Potential Incident. The incident should be investigated with the same level of intensity as if severe consequences had occurred. This focus gets everyone's attention and helps to assign appropriate corrective actions that can prevent recurrence. I believe everyone would rather proactively investigate a high potential near miss incident than investigate a tragic incident resulting in loss of life. Ensure that everyone is aware of life-critical activities and they perform the work to perfection every time.

# High Potential Incidents

In a Goal ZERO operation, fewer and fewer incidents occur, which is the good part. As the frequency of incidents declines, however, the danger lies in people relaxing and becoming complacent. We all know that learning experiences continue to occur because nothing is ever perfect.

Many companies encourage their employees to report near misses. Near miss reporting helps keep employee awareness up at all times. The problem with the near miss category is that the definition of a near miss is not typically well-defined resulting in a wide variation of reporting across the organization. If a lot of near miss incidents are reported, they don't generate a sense of urgency or receive the attention they may deserve.

I highly recommend a High Potential Incident (HPI) reporting requirement. Instituting an HPI program is extremely effective since it creates an important incident category between an actual reportable incident with consequences and a loosely defined near miss. The HPI category is a defined subset of near misses. The definition for an HPI is a near miss that had a **high probability** or **reasonable potential** of becoming a serious injury, operational, or quality incident. This classification screens out the minor near misses.

There should be a well-defined list of incidents that must be reported as an HPI. Some may be associated with non-compliance of life-critical activity requirements. Several examples are:

- *Fall from height greater than 6 feet*
- *Working at heights without proper protection*
- *Confined space entry violations*
- *Work without proper energy isolation*
- *Unprotected excavation work*
- *Breathing air incidents*
- *Any electrical shock with 120V or greater*
- *Dropped objects from heights*
- *Unexpected contact and exposure*
- *Certain defined operational incidents*

In addition to the pre-defined list of automatic HPIs, departments should report any additional incident as an HPI they deem appropriate and feel deserves increased attention.

Investigate HPIs as if the worst had happened and take appropriate measures to prevent recurrence. This approach helps to continually close gaps with expected performance and effectively demonstrates Goal ZERO expectations to the workforce: zero defects, zero non-compliance, and zero incidents. A Goal ZERO culture does not depend on luck. A focus on High Potential Incidents allows the organization to take corrective actions for serious near misses before incidents occur with significant consequences.

Designating the incident as an HPI sends a powerful message to the person who may have committed a violation and to others in the organization. Some companies might immediately terminate a person for such a violation, which may be appropriate considering the circumstances. However, short of termination, the right kind of discussion and actions with the person and the workforce can often be even more powerful and result in improved employee performance going forward.

# Investigations

I've always had a passion for reliability in our plants. I hated plant defects and incidents. I tried to treat each problem in a positive way as an opportunity to improve. Undoubtedly, a good investigation process is one of the most effective ways to drive improvement. Investigate the problem, learn from it, and take action to improve. Corrective actions apply to a department where the incident occurred and also across the company. Repeating the mistakes of others makes no sense. I wanted all our people to have fire in their guts, passion to learn from experience, and the drive to take our plants to the next level of performance.

When incidents or unintended results occur, never omit one of the most important steps in continuous improvement, conducting an investigation. Conduct the investigation as soon as possible following the event. Remain positive and keep the focus on learning and improving. Never use an investigation in a negative way by pointing fingers, lecturing, or placing blame. If needed, disciplinary action with individuals can be done later. Investigations provide an incredible coaching opportunity.

Several methodologies are available for conducting incident investigations; however, the high-level process is quite simple (and should be conducted in this order):

- *Document the facts that are associated with the incident.*
- *Determine the cause(s) of the incident.*
- *Develop action items to prevent recurrence.*

Many incident investigations take too long. Don't drag them out longer than needed. We've conducted hundreds of investigations in an hour or less. More complicated incidents take longer.

The causes of an incident can always be grouped into the categories of leadership, people, culture, systems, and assets. If you keep asking "why" in the investigation, you will eventually get to system and leadership issues. However, don't lose the value of the people, culture, and asset intermediate causes.

Data shows that roughly 90% of injuries involve some type of people element as the cause. If the incident is caused by human behavior, then careful analysis is necessary to determine if a particular individual's actions caused the incident or if broader system issues (leadership, procedures, etc.) are at play.

If a specific individual caused the incident, call it like it is. However, some leaders aren't comfortable holding individuals accountable. They assign asset or system as the root cause instead of focusing on the human behavior itself. This assignment of cause is often misguided and tends to take away from the accountability and responsibility of the individual. Be fair in your analysis, but don't keep adding more rules and punishing the entire organization for the undesired behavior or performance of a few individuals.

The final step of an investigation is to assign corrective actions to prevent recurrence. Determine if system or asset improvements are required to reduce future risk. System improvements may consist of improved leadership actions, modifications to procedures, or potential improvements to the management system. If the incident was caused purely by the actions of an individual, deal with the behavior directly with the individual following the investigation. Dealing with undesired behavior in a fair way is important in establishing a Goal ZERO culture. Don't deflect from individual responsibility by unnecessary costly asset changes or by adding additional onerous rules that impact everyone else.

A useful metric to track and communicate is the number of investigations conducted. Although counter intuitive, a higher number of investigations is better. Why? Investigating incidents means that departments are evaluating their issues and making improvements. If the number of investigations starts tracking downwards, start asking why. As incidents with consequences begin to decrease, more focus can be applied to high potential incidents and near misses. Keep learning and improving. Finally, all corrective actions must be completed by the due date, which is another aspect of the Goal ZERO philosophy.

Manufacturing organizations understand the value of investigations. Investigations document the facts, determine root causes, and develop corrective actions to prevent recurrence. Formally investigating defects and problems in many other functions is not common due to the negative implications associated with investigations. However, a culture of investigating problems is critical for continuous improvement. If the word "investigation" seems threatening in your culture, give the process another name such as "after action review," "assessment," or "analysis." The objective is to address problems directly in an adult manner and make improvements to prevent recurrence. Once you develop this cadence, you'll find it's not as painful as you might have imagined. Your organization can't afford to repeat the same mistakes over and over again.

> **GOAL ZERO NUGGET:**
> *Investigations are an essential process for achieving continuous improvement.*

# Learning from Experience Process

Many companies have a "Learning from Incidents" work process. We took learning a step further. We understood that you not only "learn from incidents," but you also learn from audits, sharing of best practices, internal improvements, individual input, external incidents, and all types of additional external information. Therefore, we changed the name to a "Learning from Experience" work process.

The Excellence Models make it easy and efficient to capture input from a variety of sources. The Excellence Model Owners review incident investigations and audits to determine areas for improvement within their section of the management system. In addition, anyone in the organization is encouraged to submit good ideas or learnings from various sources into the system which then are routed to the right Excellence Model Owner and associated team.

Here's a situation familiar to all of us. You attend a conference and learn some new information that would be extremely helpful to the company. You return to work enthusiastic about your new knowledge, but your daily workload and urgent items consume your time. The new information goes unshared and unutilized within the organization and often dies on the vine. It's a shame to not capture and take advantage of this new information. With the Learning from Experience process, it's easy to submit your learnings and ideas to the appropriate Excellence Model Owner for further consideration.

Reviewing major incidents at other companies is a vital source of learning. The Chemical Safety Board is a good source for information in the energy and petrochemical industries. Test each incident against your management system with the question, "Would proper execution of our management system have prevented this incident?" If the answer is no, make necessary improvements to the system. If the answer is yes, use the incident as an example to your organization of how important it is to follow the system. Take action as if the incident had just occurred in your organization. Always use an unfortunate incident as an opportunity to learn and improve.

The key is creating a process where learnings and information are captured and improvements are documented into your management system. Updating the system assures the learnings are not forgotten in the future.

# Gap Assessment and Gap Closure

A gap assessment and gap closure process is important for two main reasons. The first reason is for compliance when new documents in a management system are issued. New and revised documents are typically issued twice a year so the departments can plan accordingly. The responsibility of the facility is to perform a gap assessment and identify actions required to close the gaps. The department assigns action items and gap closures are tracked to completion.

The second use of the gap assessment and gap closure process is for newly acquired M&A assets. If you have developed a well-documented management system, integration of M&A

assets becomes much easier. Each newly acquired facility conducts a gap analysis for the documents in the management system and then develops and executes a gap closure plan.

The principle is that newly acquired facilities will convert to your management system for overall consistency. Of course, the newly acquired company or facilities may have some very good practices of their own. For these situations, items are entered into the Learning from Experience work process and incorporated into your existing system as appropriate. I'll explain more details later in the Mergers and Acquisitions section.

# Self-Assessment and Auditing

Three primary levels of ownership and assessment are important for full compliance with rules and regulations. The first is the personal responsibility of every employee and contractor to follow all rules. One hundred percent compliance is fundamental to a Goal ZERO culture. The second level is a regular cadence of self-assessments at each operating unit. Finally, independent audits are an important aspect of good corporate governance. No matter how good units may be, a continuous process for checking compliance is important.

Each operating unit must maintain a robust self-assessment process. Of the many mechanisms for self-assessments, my favorite is one that operates on a continuous basis, which can be accomplished through the Divide and Conquer process. Divide self-assessment accountability for standards and other mandatory requirements among the personnel in your operation, including plant operators. These assignments increase individual responsibility and improve employee engagement.

Establish expectations clearly. All employees should carefully read and thoroughly understand their assigned requirements. On a regular basis, they should perform checks to ensure the unit is complying. If they find gaps, they should correct the deficiency. If the gap is beyond their control, notify an appropriate person that can address the issue. This type of self-assessment process spreads the workload and keeps an eye on compliance at all times.

A well-designed and functioning self-assessment process is easy to manage and blends into daily work. If conducted the right way, the unit will remain in full compliance at times. If the self-assessment process is functioning as expected, independent audits will simply confirm that everything is in good shape.

Staffing independent audit teams with personnel from within your company is preferred. Your people learn more when they actively participate. Use external resources only if you don't have the expertise or enough personnel within your company. Assign individuals skilled in auditing techniques and subject matter expertise as full-time auditors. In addition to the full-time auditors, audit teams should include people from other units. I call them "guest auditors." Including guest auditors accomplishes several objectives: it provides a fresh set of eyes to identify gaps and it also serves as good learning and development for the individuals. Keep track of the guest auditors and make sure everyone has an opportunity to participate in audits of other units.

Most importantly, auditing should serve as a learning experience for everyone involved. Auditors have the benefit of learning from many different facilities and should share their learnings. The audited facility personnel and the audit team members should both learn from the experience. In addition to learning at the individual audited unit, findings and learnings from each audit should be communicated to the Excellence Model Owner for potential updating and improvement of documents in the management system.

**GOAL ZERO NUGGET:**
*A robust self-assessment process will identify most non-compliance situations.*

# The "WHY" Review

In our plants, we initially found that Operational Excellence audits were being performed, noncompliance items were found, audit reports were written, plants performed corrective actions and then business went on as usual.

Remember that in a Goal ZERO culture, every department should be in full compliance with every requirement at all times. The department should have an ongoing, robust self-assessment process to assure all items are always in compliance. If non-compliance items are discovered, it's important to determine "why" the non-compliance items existed.

To take compliance to the next level, we added an additional step to the audit process. After an audit of a unit was completed and significant non-compliance items were found, we'd conduct a follow-up meeting called the "WHY" Review. The purpose was to learn and improve. We didn't dwell on "what" the findings from the audit were. Rather, we focused on "why" the non-compliance items existed. The explanations typically resulted in a system problem or people performance (including leadership) issues. The participants in the meeting included the plant manager and anyone he or she wanted to bring from their team, the plant manager's boss, the head of Operational Excellence and myself.

Sometimes we determined a requirement in a global standard wasn't clear and needed to be updated or eliminated entirely if deemed a low priority. Other times, the conclusion was that the plant didn't have a sufficient process for assuring compliance in a particular area. At times, a non-compliance was due to an individual that simply wasn't performing his/her assigned task and needed to be dealt with individually. And finally, the non-compliance was sometimes a plant leadership issue, i.e., allowing a culture of non-compliance to exist.

Regardless of the cause, these sessions always provided a terrific learning experience and a coachable moment for leadership. These reviews were an opportunity to reinforce how serious we were about Goal ZERO compliance. The sessions were not intended to be negative towards plant leadership although I'm sure none of them looked forward to the session. Instead, the sessions served the purpose and allowed the plant managers to do some self-reflection on their leadership behavior and how they could work better with their teams to deliver desired results.

# Change Management

Building a new culture of Goal ZERO and Operational Excellence requires continuous focus and constancy of purpose. A change management process should be followed, and many processes are available. Here are the steps I like to follow for instituting effective and lasting change:

1. *Develop a Compelling Case for Change and Vision*
2. *Create a Sense of Urgency*
3. *Form a Strong Team*
4. *Establish Clear Accountability and Expectations*
5. *Communicate, Communicate, Communicate*
6. *Generate Short Term Wins*
7. *Measure Results*
8. *Sustain the Change*

Leadership in organizations often spends considerable time developing and planning change initiatives. However, by the time a program gets rolled out to the organization, leadership has already moved on to the next priority area. To be successful, leadership needs to remain intimately involved during steps 5-8 of the process.

Just as it took leadership a while to fully understand and get behind the new concepts, it will take the same amount of time for the people across your organization. Times of change are an excellent time for leaders to lead, dedicating time to coaching, talking, and listening to their people.

The second area of caution is to not underestimate the time and effort it takes to truly impact culture change. Stay the course and be consistent in your messaging at all times. Goal ZERO is a mindset and once engrained in people's minds, it won't ever go away. Don't forget to communicate frequently during every step of the change process to institute the permanent change.

# Initiative and Action Item Overload

Every initiative has good intentions, but the organization has limited capacity. Initiative overload can create too much distraction from the daily pursuit of excellence. Make sure you have a robust prioritization process to help manage the load. Someone must have the power to say "stop" and draw the line on initiatives.

The same principle applies for action items. Action items are assigned from meetings, investigations, audits, and many other initiatives. Action items are essential to correct problems or make improvements in your work. But remember, each action item creates work for someone. People have limited time and every action item will take the place of some other work that is needed.

My advice is to use strict prioritization for action items, the same as for initiatives. It's easy to proceed through a meeting or incident investigation and create action items along the way. However, at the end of the meeting or following the meeting, someone needs to review the action items in context with everything else on people's plates and cull out the ones with lower priority. Make sure people are always working on the highest value items that will deliver the most positive impact.

As mentioned before, every action item that gets assigned in a Goal ZERO culture must be performed by the assigned due date and tracked. The process should allow for extending the date based on valid reasons, but these extensions should be the exception and not the rule. Deadline extensions should be documented and monitored. With this process, you should always have zero overdue corrective actions. Overdue corrective actions create legal liabilities, not to mention how terrible it would be if someone was seriously injured because you hadn't completed corrective actions previously identified.

The bottom line is to establish a strict threshold for creation of action items, make sure someone is assigned responsibility to complete each action item and maintain a zero-overdue status at all times.

# Metrics and
# Key Performance Indicators

We all know that data is powerful. Data is used to track progress, to identify trends and potential problem areas, to improve performance and to reward people based on their performance.

We found that basic definitions of key terms are extremely important to prevent confusion. It may seem obvious, but a clear understanding of the difference between "metrics" and "key performance indicators (KPI)" by everyone is essential:

- *Metrics. These individual items are measured within a certain area of focus. The number of metrics an organization may have is limitless.*
- *Key Performance Indicators (KPI). These indicators are the critical few metrics most important to a company or a department. They can be indicators important for success or items that need special focus for improvement. KPIs can change year to year.*

At higher levels in the organization, maintain a laser focus on the KPIs and drive performance hard. As necessary, drill down into the various metrics that support each individual KPI. At lower levels in the organization, the individual metrics become much more important in driving KPI progress.

List all of the metrics that you expect to be tracked and clearly define each one. Determine how each metric will be measured and who is responsible and accountable for maintaining the metric. Don't allow any important metric to fall through the cracks.

# Data Management and Reporting

As previously discussed, the metrics tracked within each area of work can be in the hundreds. A lot of time and energy goes into collecting data. However, it's amazing how little effort is put into effectively reporting data in a meaningful way that grabs people's attention and changes behavior. I've seen many reports packed with data in complicated tables and charts. It may be the easiest way to report for the person that assembled the data, but the reader must dig into the data to understand the real "story" the data is telling.

Once again, simplification is the key. Data is powerful. To be effective, data reporting should be done in a manner that is persuasive and drives behavior. Report the data that is most important and in a manner that is clearly understood by the intended audience. Use discipline to prioritize and limit the number of metrics or KPIs reported. Arrange the data and metrics in a manner to tell the story in an intuitive manner.

We used this concept extensively when reporting Operational Excellence data. A monthly report was issued that began with a single page dashboard of Key Performance Indicators. The dashboard showed the monthly, year-to-date, and the previous two years of data for each KPI. The dashboard provided everyone with a snapshot of performance on the most important parameters.

From the dashboard, the company performance was clear but didn't provide information on individual sites. To increase visibility for the plants, we followed the dashboard with pareto charts. We included a series of pareto charts to emphasize key areas, **with only one KPI per chart.**

Take the subject of personal safety as an example. Instead of a table with information overload, a single pareto chart was extremely effective. We listed the safety performance of each site, from best to worst, on a pareto chart. The sites were color coded by quartile. This type of data reporting didn't require any discussion to deliver the intended message. The pareto chart told the story; the chart provided instant positive recognition for the best performers, highlighted the poorer performers, and indicated where additional efforts needed to be placed.

It was clear that to get off of the wrong end of the chart, a plant needed to work harder and improve performance.

Reporting data in this manner resulted in significant leader behavior change and rapid improvements. When you report data, make the intention as obvious as possible and use as many pareto charts as necessary to highlight individual important components.

The concept of showing performance results from top to bottom is no different than in sports. You can check the sports results every day and find your favorite team's status. These rankings are an incredible motivator. Think how boring sports would be if the games were played, but the scores and rankings were never communicated. No one would care and the players certainly wouldn't try as hard.

**GOAL ZERO NUGGET:**
*Data is powerful if presented in an effective manner.*

# Benchmarking

I am a huge fan of benchmarking to monitor performance relative to others and to capture best practices. In a large company, opportunities for internal benchmarking between operating units are plentiful. Benchmarking compares parameters and each unit should utilize the data constructively in their quest to become the best.

Sam Walton's benchmarking expectations called for every Walmart store manager to periodically walk through their competitor stores. The managers were expected to observe their competition's work processes and any new ideas and concepts that were emerging. Walton realized that his company didn't have all the answers and they were always interested in learning from others.

Companies such as Solomon Associates and Phillip Townsend Associates perform excellent benchmarking services throughout the refining, chemical, and energy value chain. Data in external benchmarking is often presented in quartiles of performance. I don't know about you, but my expectation was never to just be in the top quartile, my objective was to be the best.

Benchmark data for maintenance spending should be analyzed carefully. As I've discussed earlier, a poorly maintained and unreliable plant will typically have much higher maintenance spending due to unscheduled breakdown. You must maintain your assets in good shape if you are going to be the best in reliability and drive lowest cost in maintenance spending.

Leaders often see high maintenance benchmarking results and put added pressure on reducing budgets. The fact may be that poorly maintained facilities actually need to increase spending to resolve the root causes of their problems. Make sure a good analysis is performed to determine the actual causes of the higher maintenance spending so you can address the issues appropriately. You can't save your way to Operational Excellence if your assets are not in good shape.

# Mergers and Acquisitions Process for Operations

A good component of a management system for a growth company is a robust Mergers and Acquisitions (M&A) process. Mergers and acquisitions are typically conducted to expand geographic footprint, bring new technology or service to the company, expand the company's customer base, or create significant synergies.

Unfortunately, according to collated research and a recent Harvard Business Review report, the failure rate for M&A deals is an incredibly high 70-90 percent. It's important to weed out the bad projects in the due diligence process. From an operations point of view, why acquire another company unless you can operate it better? My advice is to establish a strong Operational Excellence culture with a robust management system before making acquisitions. Then you will be able to move quickly with the acquisition, integrate systems and work processes, achieve synergies, and drive value creation.

Corporate and commercial leadership typically negotiate the deals, but operating units have a major role in implementation. Synergies and expected value creation are developed and then the deal is executed. I was fortunate during my career to participate in several successful acquisitions and divestitures. Following my retirement, I worked on a project with Pilko & Associates, a leading advising and consulting organization for Operational Excellence. In advising a client on a potential major acquisition, we provided an M&A work process focused totally on operations.

The operation's M&A process has three phases:

- *Phase 1. Developing the deal, pre signing*
- *Phase 2. Detailed preparation, between signing and closing*
- *Phase 3. Executing the deal, post-closing*

Phase 1 consists of the early stages of deal preparation, when due diligence is conducted with a laser focus on valuation. Potential synergies are developed during this phase. The other important aspects of Phase 1 are risks and potential costs. One of the elements commonly missed when developing deals is the expense or capital required to close gaps with your management system requirements. The other is to determine risks with the new acquisition and whether your organization will accept those risks or not. It's much better to identify the risks and costs early, especially if they prevent the deal from going forward. It's better to know them and kill the deal rather than learning much later and having the deal destroy value.

In addition to due diligence, Phase 1 is the time to begin preparations for Phase 2. Begin to develop plans and answer questions such as how the combined company will be structured, will it be a takeover or merger of equals, who are the decision-making authorities, what are the role definitions, who are the key stakeholders, and what is the communications plan?

If the decision is made to proceed, Phase 2 begins when the deal is signed and lasts until closing. Timing for this phase is typically 6-18 months, depending on the size and complexity of the deal. Regulatory approvals will require significant resources and can add uncertainty to the actual closing date. During Phase 2, detailed preparations and decisions should be made regarding the management system, work processes, people, and assets.

If Phase 2 is executed properly, you will be able to make all necessary decisions and hit the ground running on Day 1 following deal closure. Phase 2 should be executed function by function with clear expectations for deliverables. Phase 2 is the time to:

- *Announce legal business rules (stock purchase, do's and don'ts).*
- *Create functional transition teams.*
- *Determine objectives to complete prior to Day 1.*
- *Determine preliminary asset gap closure plans.*
- *Determine standards and processes to be followed for the new organization.*
- *Review organization charts and develop headcount synergy plans.*
- *Meet the people.*
- *Determine who will fill senior leadership roles and implement soon after closing.*
- *Determine who will comprise the Phase 3 transition team.*
- *Develop detailed transition plans.*
- *Empower functional leaders; enable fast decision making.*
- *Consistently update stakeholders: employees, customers, communities, unions, and shareholders.*
- *Maintain a strong focus on safety since people may become distracted.*
- *Treat all people with dignity and respect.*
- *Move quickly, get it 80-90% right.*
- *Be ready to execute beginning on Day 1.*

Phase 3 begins when the deal closes. Phase 3 consists of executing the deal and begins with a successful Day 1. People will expect changes when the deal closes, and you should be ready to take full advantage of the "honeymoon" period. Speed in executing Phase 3 initiatives will be an important element of success. A well-planned Day 1 will set the stage for the future. Perform symbolic gestures such as installing new signs at facilities and issuing new employee badges. Create excitement with a good communications strategy and send key leaders to as many locations as possible.

On Day 1 or quickly following, make planned changes in key leadership. Make changes to the transition team and announce expectations and timing function by function. Begin to establish the new culture and expectations immediately. Conduct gap analysis and gap closure plans at the locations and then relentlessly close the gaps in a timely fashion. Acquisitions can put the entire company at risk if facilities are not integrated into the existing culture and management system. Your company is only as good as its weakest link.

I've listed only the high-level points of the Operational M&A process, but you get the idea that each phase is unique. Of course, many details are embedded within each phase. Finally, communicate often with your stakeholders throughout the process. The proper execution of each phase enables the next phase to move quicker and more efficiently. Proper execution of the M&A process will significantly improve your chances for success in expected value creation.

# CHAPTER 8

## Keeping Assets in Good Shape

This chapter is important for organizations that rely on physical equipment and tools to produce product or provide services. One of the fundamental elements of Operational Excellence is to simply "maintain the kit." Properly maintaining assets is so obvious, but equipment is often not maintained up to expectations. Major operating equipment in a manufacturing plant and the tools that are used by the workforce, must be maintained properly at all times. Operating and using equipment in poor condition is simply inexcusable. People know what needs to be done, but for whatever reason, don't do it as well as they should.

I could list hundreds of reliability, quality, safety, environmental, and value destroying incidents that were caused simply by not maintaining equipment and facilities properly. These incidents are all preventable and should never occur in a Goal ZERO culture.

Asset reliability includes selecting the desired technology, designing and constructing facilities, maintaining the equipment, and operating equipment the right way. You must strive for perfection each step of the way. Numerous defects and incidents have been caused by each of these asset aspects.

The Allyl Chloride unit, my first manufacturing job, was one of the most difficult plants to operate with hazardous materials such as propylene, chlorine, and hydrochloric acid flowing throughout the process. When I arrived, the plant had an incredibly high number of unplanned shutdowns, gas releases, and fires. Maintenance was very poor, demolition of old equipment was far behind, instruments weren't working, numerous alarms were in the active position, and excessive corrosion existed everywhere. Costs were out of control and we were always playing catchup.

My colleagues and I went to work repairing instrumentation and other equipment and working on all types of reliability improvement projects. At the same time, we revised and updated all of the operating procedures and began to develop a culture of full compliance with the operating personnel. This work took a couple of years, but we were able to transition the plant into one of the most reliable, safest, and *profitable* units across Dow. We achieved Operational Excellence through a leadership, people, culture, systems, and assets approach.

It's actually pretty basic; you must maintain your assets in good shape before you can even think about progressing further. Every detail is important. It's vital that all equipment have clear ownership with defined responsibilities. Divide and conquer as much as possible and hold people accountable.

Many types of asset reliability programs are available such as predictive, preventative maintenance (PPM), risk-based inspections, asset integrity audits, and numerous metrics and reliability tracking systems. Pick the ones that work best for you and make sure they are done to perfection.

# Controlling Costs, the Right Way

In my Allyl Chloride plant example above, we had to overspend our maintenance budget for a while to get the facility in good condition. Of course, obtaining approval required considerable discussion with supporting data. Top management may not like it, but they are generally willing to approve extra spending if they truly understand why the spending is important, believe it will make a difference and understand the consequences of not doing it.

Throughout my career, I've often seen manufacturing units that are under the responsibility of leaders with no operating experience. Some of these leaders determine how much the business can afford and set strict budgets—no excuses. I've seen some of these leaders turn down requests for extra spending even though the work was necessary. Lack of appropriate funding was one of the causes of the 2005 BP Texas City incident, in which process hazards had been identified, but insufficient funds were provided.

A similar example was in one of our joint ventures when I was Vice President of EH&S at Dow. This joint venture had been formed about five years previously and the plant manager was a good, experienced Dow person. The joint venture was operated independently of Dow and the plant manager reported directly to the business vice president, an unusual reporting relationship for Dow plants at the time.

An incident occurred in which an employee was severely burned from an equipment failure in a boiler unit. Upon investigation and follow-up discussions, we realized the joint venture was not being operated or maintained up to Dow standards. The plant manager told me how frustrated he had been since taking the job. He had told the vice president many times about the problems and the extra cost needed to get the plant up to standards. He said the vice president told him they couldn't afford it; the expense would kill the business.

The plant manager was in an unfortunate position of reporting to a bad leader; and as a result, had operated the plant in poor condition resulting in an unfortunate injury. At the time, Dow was making billions of dollars in profits. Blaming a serious injury or fatality on lack of affordability in a business unit or subsidiary wouldn't have passed the red face test. In my independent position as Vice President of EH&S, I was able to help persuade the business to provide necessary funding for the plant. I also learned to increase our independent functional audits and checks of operating units to proactively assure all were following our management system expectations and maintaining facilities in good shape.

These examples show that improperly maintaining an asset is sometimes due to the individual unit cost and profitability restraints of a particular business, not the restraints of the entire company. The business leader has his/her scorecard, which can cause conflicts with core values of the company. Through the years, I often found disconnects between the CEO of a company and the leaders of units, functions, and businesses down in the organization.

I have yet to find a good CEO who wants any of his/her units to be operated in poor condition or in an unsafe manner. This issue is another reason why manufacturing and EH&S should have strong, independent voices at the top of the organization to help resolve such conflicts of priorities.

I've also witnessed multiple occasions when a poor plant manager delayed much needed maintenance knowing that he would soon be transferred to another unit. The delayed maintenance typically involved "unseen" items such as internal equipment inspections. Later, the next manager and the company suffered much more by the reliability problems caused by the lack of proper maintenance.

In our company, we were laser focused on meeting budgets, but we were even stricter if a manager took shortcuts and neglected regularly scheduled maintenance. Eliminating this type of work was not an acceptable way to meet budget. We took a Goal ZERO approach for inspections with no overdue inspections allowed. Lack of preventative maintenance typically costs more bottom-line dollars later due to the unscheduled downtime and lost sales that occur.

Having said all of this, don't get me wrong. I have always had a relentless focus on cost control as it is essential for profitability and competitiveness. We always strived to be the low-cost producer and be prepared for downturns in the economic cycle. In cyclical businesses, your company and all of your competitors continue to get better. Therefore, during good times and to prevent cost increases, we kept our budget focused on the bottom of the economic cycle so that we didn't need to make drastic cuts during the next downturn.

However, the difference between necessary spending and wasteful spending is huge. Improving efficiency of maintenance processes and strict prioritization are essential. Invest time to evaluate the systems and processes to gain a full understanding before blindly setting cost budgets.

In closing this section, I made a statement one time that I heard repeated over the following years, "We are committed in the race to make this a great company, but we are not going to do it on bad tires!" It's true. Maintain your assets in good shape if you are truly interested in achieving Operational Excellence.

**GOAL ZERO NUGGET:**
*Cost control must be conducted
in the right manner.*

# Prioritization

When I worked in The Netherlands, I was a member of the site maintenance steering team. We had been driving improved maintenance procedures and practices and successfully lowering maintenance spending. One of the ethylene plant managers came into our meeting and gave a passionate presentation. He claimed that some of his ethylene piping had too much corrosion, was unsafe and he didn't have enough budget to do the maintenance. I was upset and concerned about his safety comments, so I told him I wanted to go look at the piping following the meeting.

As we drove into the entrance of his unit, we saw eight maintenance people painting everything along the entrance to the plant. The equipment that they were painting looked fine to me, but the Dutch have a lot of pride and like their facilities to be perfect. I asked him if this work was out of the same budget that he had for his "unsafe" ethylene piping. Of course, it was, and then we had a short discussion about prioritization. After talking for a while, he said, "You don't need to go look at the piping, we'll get it painted." He finally realized he really wasn't prioritizing and doing the most important work first.

# Protecting Equipment

Following an incident, many people will assign the root cause to "equipment failure." If you dig deep enough, however, you may find that the work process or procedure to maintain and operate the equipment was insufficient. Even more often, the cause of equipment failure may be human behavior; failing to properly perform the work process or procedure for maintenance or operation of the equipment.

Numerous industry examples of "asset" problems are actually caused by gaps in the "system" or from individual "people" actions. And of course, they can all be traced back to leadership issues. A few examples include:

- *Pump seal failures are sometimes caused by mis-operation such as dead heading the pump or excessive cavitation. Machinists complain over and over that the operator is abusing the pump. (People)*
- *Gas releases or fires caused by corrosion under insulation catch far too many companies by surprise. Proper inspection frequencies and attention to detail in the inspections are essential to preventing these types of incidents. (People, System)*
- *Damaged trays in distillation towers are a common occurrence. Sometimes this damage might be caused by excessive corrosion or vibration, but far too many times it's the result of the liquid layer getting too far up in the column or blowing out the trays during startup. (People, System)*
- *Equipment often fails because it simply hasn't been lubricated according to the schedule. (People)*
- *An airplane won't survive very long if the pilot doesn't know how to operate it. (People, System)*

Process equipment and tools will normally operate well and reliably if they are maintained as recommended and operated properly. Often, a leadership or people element is one of the causes of equipment failure: possibly due to improper training, the individual being careless or making a mistake, or the person simply choosing to operate the equipment in an incorrect manner.

Regardless of the reason, it's important to be disciplined in investigations and do not hesitate to identify people or leadership as a cause that led to an incident. People will respond and work in a Goal ZERO manner if the expectations are clear, they have the right tools and training and they are held accountable for their actions. This is fair. Don't sugar coat it when human behavior, including leadership, is a contributing cause to an incident. Call it like it is.

# Exceptional Housekeeping

Exceptional housekeeping is a cornerstone of a Goal ZERO operation. Housekeeping should be a basic tenet for every person in the organization, from CEO to the front-line operator.

In one of my early assignments in Dow's Texas Operations, the unit's housekeeping was terrible, and the unit manager didn't care. Therefore, many people in the unit didn't care about it either; but the sloppy housekeeping bothered me. Around that same time, I remember taking our children to Disneyland and marveling at the wonderful housekeeping in the park. I saw employees immediately picking up any litter that hit the ground and clipping the edges of grass immaculately. I knew the difference between Disneyland housekeeping and what we were tolerating in the unit was leadership expectations.

Shortly after our Disneyland visit, a new site manager, Larry Wright, was assigned to Texas Operations. He insisted that every unit in the site maintain excellent housekeeping. I was thrilled, and we began to immediately clean up our plant. You could see the pride and morale improve along with the cleanup. Larry demonstrated the power of strong leadership.

From that moment on, I accelerated my passion for excellence in housekeeping. We conducted a 15 minute "bucket brigade" in all of my plants once per week immediately after lunch. Everyone participated. I made it a point to personally cover as much area as I could to be visible to as many employees and contractors as possible. The bucket brigade made a big impression on everyone and our housekeeping was always second to none.

Another example was on one of my visits to China. I went to a unit our company had acquired in a large industrial complex owned by another company. The housekeeping was very poor, nothing was painted, and weeds were growing everywhere. I talked to employees at the unit and convinced them to clean up and to send pictures to me. They followed my guidance and the improvement over the next few months was remarkable. In later months, to my delight, they said the units around them, owned by the other company, began to take notice and were actively working to improve their areas too. Peer pressure works.

One of our plant managers in France and a good friend of mine, Jerome Mauvigney, coined the phrase "the Smolik

Sweep." He said every time I visited the plant and we walked around, I would casually reach down as we were walking and pick up any piece of trash that I saw. I always felt it was a good way to set a good example and demonstrate our expectations. I chuckled each time on these tours as other people in our group would start picking up litter too.

Good housekeeping is important for contractors working in your operation. If the work area is cluttered when they begin their work, they will leave the site in even worse condition. However, if they start with a clean workplace, they will leave it clean.

Begin by making sure that exceptional housekeeping is an expectation across your company. Place trash containers in convenient locations throughout the unit and keep them emptied out on a regular basis. A good guideline is that nothing should be on the ground unless it's there for a specific reason. Keep areas painted and well lit.

Housekeeping is important in so many ways. It builds employee pride. Housekeeping is integral to safety and quality performance. It helps with recruiting when potential employees see an exceptional looking workplace. The public sees it. Customers love good housekeeping. And most importantly, outstanding housekeeping is a visible sign of a Goal ZERO culture.

**GOAL ZERO NUGGET:**
*Good housekeeping is*
*fundamental for excellence.*

# Out of Sight, Out of Mind

Another common problem of asset failure is equipment and process units that are "out of sight, out of mind." I'm referring to basic, important support equipment such as air compressors, cooling towers, wastewater treatment facilities and many other similar services. Similar to electrical power and water supply in your homes, people take these necessities for granted until they aren't available, and then it becomes a serious problem.

This type of support equipment is often assigned to a junior person in the plant. The person may not have the proper skills or doesn't truly understand the severe consequences that could occur if the equipment fails. The equipment operates well for a period of time and then experiences a failure, typically due to neglect for too long and improper maintenance.

A typical example in warm climates are instrument air compressors. The humidity of the air is not so critical during warm weather and people believe they are operating just fine. However, when a hard freeze comes along, the moisture in the instrument air freezes and disables critical instruments. That's when disaster strikes. I've seen incidents occur like this many times across industry. Proper operation of instrument air compressors, like other critical equipment, must be maintained in good shape at all times.

Just like tying your shoes in the John Wooden example, every small detail is important for an operating unit. "Out of sight, out of mind" equipment is as important as the primary operating equipment. It's okay to assign the responsibility to a younger person if there is a good management system of procedures, standards, training, metrics, inspection, maintenance, self-assessment, and auditing. No excuse is adequate for auxiliary equipment failing due to improper operation and maintenance.

**GOAL ZERO NUGGET:**
*Never allow "out of sight"*
*equipment to fall into disrepair.*

# CHAPTER 9

## The Goal ZERO Roadmap for Operational Excellence

While writing this book, I created a Goal ZERO Roadmap by reviewing our past experiences and actions that led to Operational Excellence. We had many false starts and stops along the way. By following the Roadmap, you can benefit from our experiences and accelerate your progress. Don't reinvent the wheel; build on what is already working in your company. Focus your time on those areas that need improvement. At the end, you will have a management system that fits your culture and drives improvement.

The Roadmap will help create an inspired vision, develop a Goal ZERO culture, improve your Operational Excellence management system and drive towards excellence. The Roadmap is structured around the formula I have shown several times:

**Operational Excellence =**
**Leadership + People + Culture + Systems + Assets**

The size of your company or how far along you are with Operational Excellence doesn't matter; you can fill in the gaps to accelerate your progress. The Roadmap is helpful for both manufacturing companies and services providers; the principles are the same. The purpose is to provide a guide based on proven practices and to stimulate your thinking.

While no single silver bullet will deliver Operational Excellence, all major change initiatives begin with leadership. Results focused leaders begin by assuring that a system is in place and followed. This system builds on best practices, drives out variation and assures that all of the necessary elements are aligned and are executed to perfection on a consistent basis. The goal of the organization is to build on this consistency to achieve excellence in everything. It's all about working smarter, working more efficiently, unleashing the talents of people, and achieving higher levels of excellence.

Operational Excellence begins with leadership that is committed to achieving excellence on a sustained basis. Leaders at all levels must articulate their vision for excellence, explain why it is important and lead the way through their actions. Leaders must have constancy of purpose and not waver in their commitment. People throughout the organization need to align and believe that achieving Goal ZERO performance and Operational Excellence are indeed possible. Leaders need to not only exert their personal power and ability to influence others, but also must implement a cadence of activities and a management system that is predictable and delivers results. A robust management system provides corporate oversight and consistency. For a larger company, the system needs to be at a high enough level for local sites and locations to adapt and add more details for their local situation. If you are building a management system for a smaller company or a single location, your system needs to capture the items significant for your operation. If you are a single contributor in your company, share these guidelines with your peers and work together to develop a good functioning management system in your area of activity.

A quality management system takes time to develop. Remember, "The best time to plant an oak tree is 20 years ago. The second-best time is today." The same is true for establishing and executing a good management system. It's never too late to do the right thing. Begin today.

Assign an individual to lead the Operational Excellence change initiative with clear expectations and accountability. If your organization is large enough, a multi-functional steering team is highly recommended. Operational Excellence is not just an Operations or EH&S responsibility, it takes all major functions working together. Breaking down and eliminating functional silos and barriers is critical.

I won't mislead you. This journey is a lot of work and you should go at a pace that your resources can manage. Deliver some quick wins that will energize the organization. Your people will appreciate the improved clarity and elimination of confusion. Consistency of purpose and keeping focused on the prize will yield benefits quickly.

The improvement process for Operational Excellence is overwhelming to most people, but it doesn't have to be. The following 10 Step Roadmap describes the major components for developing, executing, and continually improving a good system. The Roadmap will help people to understand how each step fits into the big picture. I've listed the items in the best order I could, but it's not a linear process. Each element is important for the system to work. Here is the Roadmap:

### The Goal ZERO Roadmap for Operational Excellence

1. *Define the* **Case for Change and a Clear Vision for the Future.**
2. *Establish a* **Goal ZERO Mentality.** *Full compliance, zero defects.*
3. *Develop a set of* **Operational Excellence Expectations.**
4. *Create the framework for your* **Operational Excellence Management System.**
5. **Digitize the System** *to connect people and the system to accelerate improvement.*
6. **Assign the Right People** *to develop the Excellence Models. Establish clear roles and responsibilities for developing, updating, and utilizing the Excellence Models.*
7. **Build the Excellence Models** *and* **Simplify Documentation.**
8. **Roll Out to the Organization** *to develop gap closure plans at each location.*
9. *Drive progress through the* **Leadership, People, Culture, Systems, and Assets** *techniques.*
    a. **Leadership** *creates the vision, inspires the organization, and drives improvement.*
    b. **People** *are well trained and execute the system.*
    c. *A* **Goal ZERO culture** *sets the norms for behavior*
    d. *The* **System** *documents best practices for technology, standards, work processes, procedures, tools, templates, and reference information.*
    e. **Assets** *are well designed and maintained.*
10. **Execute and Continually Update the System.**

# 1. The Case for Change and a Clear Vision

Most people are naturally reluctant to embrace change. The reluctance can come from any area of the organization: front line operators, supervisors, department managers, and C-suite leaders. People are busy and focused on other initiatives. They don't trust that the change will work, so they don't want to put in the extra effort. A common question is, "What's in it for me?"

Creating a good case for change and addressing the concerns of all parties is critical. People are more willing to accept change if they understand "why" it's important and the benefits it will bring.

Change takes energy. Change is sometimes expensive. You must either have a major discomfort with your current state or have a clear vision for taking your organization to the next level of performance

Therefore, the beginning of any major change management initiative involves creating a compelling case for change. The context for change is important. Are you fighting complacency from consistent yet mediocre performance, or are you responding to a recent serious incident? Why are you implementing the change? What is your vision for the future? What problems are you trying to solve? Different people get motivated in different ways.

As a leader, you will encounter all kinds of excuses. "We don't have the people to do this work, we don't have the budget, we have other priorities, and we don't have the time," I've heard them all. These excuses remind me of the person that was chopping wood with a dull axe and someone suggested that he sharpen the axe. He responded, "I don't have time."

The choice is clear; do you want to continue inefficiently, or do you want to take a step to become better organized so you can accelerate progress? I would much rather spend the time developing a good system to prevent defects rather than endlessly investigating problems over and over. You will figure out how to prioritize and get the job done if you have the right tone at the top and achieving Operational Excellence is important to your organization,

It's relatively easy to develop a case for change for Operational Excellence. Poll your people for their input on the problems they face and ideas that could make the organization better. People don't have much difficulty coming up with what is wrong. I'll bet you can recognize and relate to some of the following statements that make a compelling case for change:

- *Too many people are getting hurt.*
- *Reliability is not what we expect.*
- *We have too many customer quality incidents.*
- *Operational problems occur in one area while the solution is very well known elsewhere.*
- *Repeat incidents occur from the same root causes.*
- *We don't have a good system to capture best practices.*
- *We are not fully utilizing best practices in all areas.*
- *Rules and requirements are too long and complicated.*
- *We keep reinventing the wheel and working on the same issue in different places.*
- *We are too people dependent and we lose knowledge when key people retire or leave.*

All of these issues can be resolved with good leadership and a good management system. Make your own list that summarizes your case for change. Once you have clarified the case for change, it's time to develop your vision for Operational Excellence. You essentially want to create a robust management system that captures the knowledge from inside and outside of the company and is utilized efficiently and effectively by all. People respond to future focus when they understand clearly what you are trying to accomplish and more importantly, what it will look like.

A few bullet points that will help turn your current problems into vision elements for improving Operational Excellence are:

- *Fewer people will get hurt.*
- *Operations will become more consistent and predictable.*
- *Employee engagement and commitment will increase.*
- *Costs will decrease.*
- *All facilities will operate with best practices.*
- *We will become best in class suppliers to our customers.*

- *We will achieve consistent performance across all facilities.*
- *Redundancy and duplication of work at sites will be reduced.*
- *We will spend less time investigating incidents and more time on incident prevention.*
- *We will have a consistent framework for documenting the management system.*
- *Information and knowledge will be easy to access.*
- *Expectations will be clear and well-understood.*
- *Documents will be crisp, clear, and easy to understand.*
- *We will have succinct rules, standards, and work processes.*
- *We will have a light touch from corporate with more detail at the sites.*
- *We will eliminate confusion.*
- *We will win*

In summary, leadership must create a strong vision based on Operational Excellence, which means operating safely, reliably, consistently, and cost efficiently. Desire and expect to become the best in your industry. Approach Operational Excellence in all that you do through an integrated management system. The reward will be Goal ZERO performance, world-class reliability and significantly increased financial value. All departments, employees, and contractors have clear roles and responsibilities in the management system. Differentiate your company from all other companies through flawless execution.

**GOAL ZERO NUGGET:**
*A dynamic case for change creates excitement in any organization.*

## 2. Goal ZERO Mentality

Your organization will fundamentally change forever with the adoption of the methodology described in this book. However, the most important component is to establish a Goal ZERO mentality from the very beginning. Goal ZERO needs to be strong, firm, consistent, and resonate from the top of the organization.

The philosophy behind Goal ZERO was discussed in Chapter 1. Most important, you must decide if Goal ZERO is just a slogan or if you really plan to walk the talk. There are many companies with various types of Goal ZERO slogans, but they don't follow through to deliver the results. If it's just going to be a slogan, don't waste your time.

One of the fundamental tenants of Goal ZERO is zero non-compliance with requirements. Zero non-compliance means following 100% of the requirements, 100% of the time. In an organization that isn't strong on following rules, people start to decide for themselves which rules are important and which ones are not. Countless safety, quality, and reliability incidents during the years could have been prevented if the individual had been operating equipment properly, following the procedure correctly, wearing the required personal protective equipment and avoiding distractions.

Communicate the Goal ZERO concept at every opportunity. Use Goal ZERO terminology in your daily discussions. Talk about Goal ZERO behavior, Goal ZERO performance, and Goal ZERO expectations. Conduct discussion sessions and workshops in the workplace as I've previously discussed. It takes time for new concepts to sink in for people. Stay the course and be consistent.

## 3. Operational Excellence Expectations

Step 3 of the Goal ZERO Roadmap is to develop an **Operational Excellence Expectations Document** as described in Chapter 2. The creation of an Expectations Document is a great opportunity to gain alignment and state leadership's specific expectations in plain language in a single document. Each expectation should be written in a clear and positive manner. Operational Excellence Expectations are the minimum requirements that apply to all employees and contractors. Leaders, employees, and contractors must comply with all expectations.

Once your document is complete, print the expectations in a pamphlet and distribute to all your employees and contractors. The document provides an excellent platform for employee discussions. Discuss your vision for achieving Operational Excellence in all that you do. Take a Goal ZERO approach to each of the Expectations listed. By constant messaging and with leadership totally aligned, you will experience a rapid shift in employee mindset and level of compliance. This communication helps your workforce to understand the company's objectives and why they are important.

It's relatively easy to write a document and then put it on the shelf. To prevent this from occurring, survey every employee as to adherence to each Expectation every time a particular site or department receives an Operational Excellence audit. Separate responses from the supervision and from the employees of the audited department. As you can imagine, if the answers between the two groups are different, you have something for further discussion. Make sure everyone is committed to achieving the Expectations you have established.

## 4. Operational Excellence Management System

This section and the next two (Digitization of the System and The Right People with Clear Accountability) go hand in hand. The power is in the combination of the structure of each Excellence Model, the enabling Operational Excellence software system, and the right people with the proper skills and guidance. This combination provides an integrated platform for organizing documents, creating ease of access, improving contribution from experts, and continual use and updating of the system.

Begin by creating the framework for your management system as described in Chapter 6. Determine the appropriate management system categories and the associated Excellence Models that should be developed. Focus on a few categories and Excellence Models to get started; you can add more as the process gains momentum. An Excellence Model should be developed for the sub processes of each global category in which all documentation, information, and collective knowledge is stored and maintained. The Excellence Models are organized in a consistent manner for ease of access and utilization. Each Excellence Model looks and feels the same so people in the organization become comfortable and competent in using the system.

A good functioning management system provides a consistent platform for leaders to lead and focus on execution. The system gets everyone on the same page regarding requirements and procedures. Consistent terminology and vocabulary are critical to avoid confusion in the organization, especially if you conduct business in countries with different native languages. Providing clarity and ease of understanding are motivational to the organization.

Once the company-wide system is in place, locations can build on the framework and add details for how they operate locally. The end result for the user in the field is a system that includes corporate and local requirements in an easy to use, aligned manner.

## 5. Digitization of the System

Throughout this book, I describe methods for creating business value, improving quality, reducing customer incidents, enhancing safety performance, assuring compliance, and inspiring your workforce. To enhance and enable the efficiency, effectiveness, and execution of your management system, a well-functioning Operational Excellence software system is essential. Today's software technology can become a differentiating factor in your operations and with your customers.

Your organization, like all others, has a significant amount of information organized in many different ways. The key to a good functioning management system is to organize your documentation in a way that makes it accessible by the people when they need it.

Bill Gates wrote a book entitled *Business @ the Speed of Thought*. I've always thought it's the perfect title for how we should conduct our business efficiently through the utilization of a good management system and excellent software technology. The technology exists such that people should always be able to access the prioritized information they need and then quickly execute their work. People shouldn't waste time looking for information and trying to interpret it or determine what is most important. People shouldn't repeat the same mistakes of others or fail to capture value creating opportunities that others have identified.

Countless numbers of software systems for industry are available on the market today. Most companies have software systems that store documents, collect data, manage information, and help you communicate. Each one of these software systems serves its particular purpose, but how often has it been developed from the user's perspective? Is it easy to use and intuitive for the user to find the information they need quickly? Is the information updated on a regular basis? Does the software serve as an enabler for your management system and provide real time feedback?

As we worked through our journey of achieving Operational Excellence, we realized that to achieve "Business @ the Speed of Thought," we needed to have an aligned set of software systems. It is essential to make information and data accessible, and work across functions. We wanted a system that would digitize and enhance our management system to drive performance improvement. We brainstormed the characteristics for "the perfect software system" to aid in achieving Operational Excellence.

We evaluated the most popular public internet sites such as Google, Amazon, Facebook, and Twitter to determine why they were successful. These sites don't require special training and are intuitive for the users, which is why they are so widely used. Software systems for industry should have the same characteristics.

Some important elements of a perfect Operational Excellence software system are:

- *Provides a portal for all information*
- *Is intuitive and user friendly*
- *Is searchable*
- *Is cost effective*
- *Integrates with other systems*
- *Is fit for purpose: corporate level, site, or department level*
- *Breaks down barriers between functions: operations, EH&S, quality, human resources, etc.*
- *Connects people with other people*
- *Enhances compliance assurance*
- *Provides data analytics*
- *Utilizes artificial intelligence to speed progress*
- *Utilizes statistics to help drive desired behaviors*
- *Enables continuous updating and approval of the management system*
- *Generates management reports*
- *Increases accountability of subject matter experts and users*
- *Prioritizes information for the user*
- *Creates effective document control and records management*
- *Allows alignment of local and corporate mandatory requirements, preferred practices, and guidance documents*

A good software system must be designed with the users in mind and the information each person in the organization needs to do his/her job. Document creators and Excellence Model Owners have a single place for receiving new information and documenting their work product. Users in the field have a single source of truth for information they need and can find it quickly.

The system serves as a portal for other existing software tools that store information. A good software system integrates management system documentation, previous incident and audit reports, performance data, chat functions, and employee information in an easy-to-use manner. People are incorporated in the system by aligning and connecting owners, teams, subject matter experts, and interested users associated with a particular Excellence Model. Everyone in the organization has the capability to submit ideas, suggestions, and new information into the system directed at the right individuals. This type of software system proves immensely valuable in keeping the management system continually updated.

Realtime statistical and benchmark data on specific behavioral aspects and their relationship on performance helps drive the right behaviors in leaders and people across the organization. Statistics help identify the specific behaviors that drive performance improvement. Online evaluations by users of management system documents keep document writers linked to user demands and feedback.

An integrated Operational Excellence software tool that matches and enables the execution of your Operational Excellence Management System is powerful. By digitizing the elements of leadership, people, culture, systems, and assets, a good functioning software system enhances the ability of people to conduct "Business @ the Speed of Thought" and drive rapid transformation.

**GOAL ZERO NUGGET:**
*Digitization technology can be a significant process enabler.*

## 6. The Right People with Clear Accountability

Step 6 of the Roadmap is to establish roles and responsibilities for development and maintenance of the Excellence Models. It's critical that the Excellence Model Owners and teams are aligned on expectations *from the very beginning*. Clear expectations will determine how subject matter experts approach their job and the work product they deliver.

Assign an overall coordinator for the Operational Excellence Management System for the company. The coordinator is vital to keep progressing in a consistent manner. The coordinator coaches the Excellence Model

Owners and their teams so they continue to deliver products consistently and meet desired expectations.

**The roles to be filled are:**

- ***Excellence Model Owner.*** *This individual has the sole ownership of the Excellence Model. If more than one person owns it, nobody owns it.*
- ***Excellence Model Team.*** *Each Excellence Model has a team that works with the owner to develop and maintain the Excellence Model. The members of the team are expected to "do work and contribute" and not just attend meetings.*
- ***Excellence Model Extended Network.*** *The network is a group of interested individuals for the particular topic. The Extended Network is used for communications and collaboration.*
- ***Site Excellence Model Focal Point.*** *This individual at each site is responsible and accountable for transferring the Excellence Model information to the site. These individuals functionally report to the Operational Excellence Leader at the site.*

In almost all cases, these roles are part time for the individuals listed above. Use caution to not create additional full-time functional overhead. In smaller organizations, the teams may not be necessary and individuals can fill the roles for multiple Excellence Models.

Coaching of the Excellence Model Teams is important, especially in the beginning. Provide the teams with regular feedback, provide examples of what good looks like and evaluate their work. Be serious about getting each Excellence Model right and fit for purpose. It's important to create each document in the same format and follow simplicity guidance.

Unfortunately, some individuals may be the best expert in a particular field, but they may not be good at documenting and organization. In this case, don't allow the individual to be the Excellence Model Owner. Find the right person that can deliver a work product that will be widely accepted and utilized by the organization. Regularly review the performance of each team and change out members who don't contribute their fair share.

Track the progress of each Excellence Model team. Assign due dates to keep progress moving and to develop a sense of urgency. Excellence Model team agendas should be proactively created to review and update the various documents in the Excellence Model.

Provide appropriate recognition for the Excellence Model Owners and teams. Their work will have a lasting impact and each Excellence Model will contribute to the overall success of the organization.

## 7. Simplify Documentation and Build the Excellence Models

Step 7 of the Roadmap for Operational Excellence is to simplify documentation and populate each of the Excellence Models as described in Chapter 6. The Excellence Model Owners and associated teams conduct this work. However, it's not as simple as loading up the Excellence Models with numerous documents. The real value is for the teams to strictly prioritize the documents that get included in the Excellence Model, prioritize the content in each document, simplify each document and assure that the system is meeting expectations across the company.

These Excellence Models will become the foundation for your management system and each document needs to meet expectations. If you allow every Excellence Model Owner to independently develop his/her Excellence Model, there won't be any consistency. Do it the right way from the beginning.

Prioritization is vitally important. By prioritizing the content in the Excellence Model, you guide the organization to keep its focus on the most important aspects within the model and increase effectiveness and value creation. It doesn't make sense to spend much time on items of lesser importance.

As I look back on my career, one of the most impactful accomplishments, undoubtedly, was simplifying the company's standards and work processes and then organizing them so that users could easily access the information. We essentially updated every mandatory standard that applied to operations. We shortened them, made them easier to read, included only requirements that were truly mandatory, and we expected full compliance. The documents became user friendly.

The Excellence Model Owner and associated Excellence Model Team should drive clarity and simplicity. Simplification seems so obvious but is often missing within highly technical organizations. Three primary steps are important to accomplish simplification:

1. *Prioritize and minimize the **number** of documents in the Excellence Model.*
2. *Prioritize and minimize document content.*
3. *Simplify how each document is written.*

Your experts will spend considerable time generating subject matter material and hopefully do a good job of prioritizing. Therefore, it makes sense to take the next step and create documents that are easy to read and comprehend.

Simplification is so important that I spent considerable time in Chapter 6 on simplification concepts. Make sure your people read and follow the guidelines described in the chapter. Simplified systems begin with documents that are concise, clear, and easy to understand. Good documents use consistent terminology, use "shall" and "should" statements appropriately, and are written in a clear, understandable manner. Finally, each document should be measured by the Flesch Reading Ease Score.

## 8. Roll Out to the Organization

Two important stakeholder groups have work to do in the Operational Excellence Roadmap. The first group is the technical organization that develops and improves the management system and Excellence Model documents. The second group includes the operating units that must use and comply with the new and revised documents.

Communication is essential during every step of the process. Bring the organization along and ensure there aren't any surprises. The best leaders plan their work months and years into the future. Give the operating units plenty of advance notice of upcoming documents.

Rolling out the Excellence Models and associated documentation will come several months after management and the technical teams begin their work. It's important to go through the same early communications with the broader organization. Answer questions such as: why are we doing this, what is the case for change, what is the vision for the future, what will it look like and what's in it for me?

A good practice is to roll out new and revised documents on a scheduled basis. Don't wait until all documents are completed and then "dump" them on the organization. Roll out new documents on a bi-annual basis to make it more orderly for the receiving departments. Each receiving department should review the new documents and assure a gap-analysis is performed. The site should identify gaps and develop corrective actions, which are listed in an action item register.

Provide flexibility in assigning due dates for the action items. Plants are typically given up to a year to close the gaps. More time is given if capital projects are required. Approach the rollout and gap closure as a major, multi-year project.

Don't underestimate the amount of work required. However, if you communicate well and begin with a solid, well-paced schedule, you will get the work done. In the end, you'll be glad that you did. Your departments will have a much better understanding of expectations and requirements which will significantly improve their ability to comply.

# 9. Leadership, People, Culture, Systems and Assets

Nothing is simple about any of our businesses. To be successful, thousands of details must be managed well every day. However, it is important to take all of these details and organize them into a succinct communication package so that people can understand the big picture. Clarity for the organization is essential.

Step 9 of the Operational Excellence Roadmap consists of providing this clarity and driving daily progress. You should state that everything falls into one or more of the following categories: Leadership, People, Culture, Systems, and Assets. Once the people in the organization understand these concepts, going into further details becomes easier. Use these categories to be proactive in the execution of your management system to prevent incidents.

The concepts are actually quite simple. Leadership sets the direction and leads the organization. The system defines "how we do things around here." Once the system and Goal ZERO culture are in good shape, it's up to the people to execute the system. People executing the system well or poorly is the primary differentiator between mediocre and winning teams. And finally, assets are such an important element in manufacturing companies that it deserves its own category.

Each of these components must work well to achieve Operational Excellence. It's not one or the other, but all of them. Operational Excellence requires leadership, people, culture, systems, AND assets; it's the power of AND. It's pretty basic; if you have a good system and keep your assets in good shape, you can focus most of your time on the performance of your people.

## 10. Execute and Continually Update the System

Nothing is finer than a well-run organization, operating to perfection on a regular basis. People enjoy their work and are excited about the future. People have pride in the organization. Clarity and lack of confusion prevail. The culture is one of always doing things right and winning. The performance of the organization continues to reach new levels of excellence on a routine basis.

Daily execution of a fit for purpose management system can result in this type of organization. Many companies have strategies, plans, and a management system, but they don't do a good job of execution. They do a poor job of connecting the dots. By following the guidance in this chapter, people will want to use the system because it makes their job easier rather than more complicated. As they learn to operate consistently, they will execute better and better.

Step 10 of the Roadmap consists of flawless execution and continually updating the system. To ensure the system is dynamic and continually updated, use the Plan-Do-Check-Act continuous improvement cycle, commonly known as the Deming Cycle. The cycle is simple, and it works well. The Deming Cycle provides a focus for implementation of the system and delivers a format for continuous updating and improvement of documentation in the system. The cycle is also an easy way to segment the different phases of your management system and evaluate how well each is functioning.

A summary of the cycle is:

- *Plan. The plan is the starting point: A Goal ZERO culture, a good management system, a well-conceived strategy, trained people, and assets are in place. An analogy would be a football team, ready to play a game. You have your system in place, the assets are in good shape, and the people are prepared and ready to play and win the game. The plan determines what you are going to do and how you are going to do it.*
- *Do. You execute the system in this step and conduct your work. In business terms, you produce the product or deliver the services of your company. People follow the procedures, practices and work processes they have been trained on.*
- *Check. You measure the results. You have a system of metrics and key performance indicators to monitor every aspect of your operation. You perform proactive assessments, audits, and inspections to assure everything is in good shape. You investigate when defects occur or desired results are not achieved.*
- *Act. You take action to improve the system based on learnings. Improvements can be implemented in any aspect of the leadership, people, culture, systems, and assets categories. Reward and recognize people for good performance. Communicate with the organization frequently. Document learnings and improvements continuously.*

Populate each step of the Plan-Do-Check-Act cycle with topics you wish to emphasize. The cycle provides a good visual for people in your organization. Results focused leaders help their people connect the dots and see how their work fits into the big picture. When people understand the big picture, they become more motivated in conducting their work in a Goal ZERO manner.

The Plan says you are prepared and ready to go. Your team has the leadership, people, culture, technology, expectations, standards, work processes and assets necessary to win. Your technology is strong, your people are prepared, and you are ready to execute.

Execution of the management system (Do) is where you spend most of your time. It's the most important step of the cycle and determines whether you win or lose. As I've mentioned many times, the key to effective execution is good, well maintained assets, simple processes that are followed at all times, and competent, well trained and motivated people.

To achieve consistency and continually improve, everyone must adhere to the management system. By eliminating variation, you can build on historical knowledge and continually improve. Following the system will help eliminate defects, protect people, and deliver desired results.

Leadership needs to believe in the management system, continually enforce adherence at all times and consistently articulate the Goal ZERO vision. If the system has been developed in a logical and non-overbearing manner, people will readily follow it. Excellence in execution must be a core element of winning company's culture.

The "Check" step of the cycle is all about performance monitoring. The commonly used quotes are true: "You get what you measure," and "You get what you inspect, not what you expect." Hopefully, most performance monitoring is performed in a proactive manner, with regular performance reviews, checking and inspecting equipment, self-assessments, tracking performance through all kinds of performance metrics, and auditing.

However, nothing is perfect, and sub-par results or incidents occur from time to time. It's important to investigate every incident or defect to determine what went wrong and to assign action items to prevent recurrence. Never accept the excuse of not having enough time to properly investigate an incident.

Benchmarking is a key aspect of the Check step. In large companies, you have the ability to benchmark performance between internal operating units. In addition, extensive benchmarking is conducted across the industry. You can always learn from others.

Roll up the learnings from the Check step activities into your "Learning from Experience" work process. Continually identify improvement opportunities by measuring, auditing, investigating, benchmarking, and learning from others. Winston Churchill said it well, "Those who fail to learn from history are condemned to repeat it."

Regular monitoring of human performance in the Check step assures that people are doing their jobs as expected and highlights individuals that need improvement. It also provides efficiency and quality measures of performance and points out areas that will enhance excellence in performance.

An annual management system review is essential in the Check step. Take the appropriate amount of time to evaluate the entire system for effectiveness. Is the management system delivering the intended results? Are people following the system? Are changes needed for improvement? A good management system review will keep your organization headed in the right direction.

"Act" is the final step of the continuous improvement cycle. It is essential to perform all action items and strategic plans in a timely manner. It's critical to continually evaluate the big picture and developing trends. The Act step is where the best leaders create value; they play at a high enough level to determine what is not performing well in the system and adjust when necessary.

Going back to football as an example, how many times have you seen a team go into halftime with a losing score and then come out for the second half looking like a totally different team? The successful coaches understand their system and don't start over from scratch; they make minor adjustments as necessary to improve their execution, and they win. They act on the learnings!

Many company leaders admit they don't do a good job of updating the documents in their management system. The causes vary: lack of ownership, not high enough priority, no overall program for continuous improvement, etc.

The solution to this problem is making the Excellence Model Owners and Excellence Model Teams an active part of the Check and Act steps of the continuous improvement process. The teams are required to review incidents (especially major incidents from other companies) related to their area of expertise and test them against the Excellence Models.

The owners and teams should ask the question, "Would proper execution of our management system have prevented this incident?" If not, action items should be assigned to update a standard or work process in the system to correct the deficiency. Corrective actions should not only focus on a particular unit but on the corporation as a whole. This process keeps the system alive and continually improved based on the Learning from Experience work process.

It's easy to see and understand why Plan-Do-Check-Act is called the continuous improvement cycle. If done well, it represents clearly to everyone how the management system functions and will help people connect the dots. By focusing on each step of the cycle, you will indeed continuously improve. Individual roles, responsibilities, and accountability are essential for every step in a management system.

And again, have I mentioned communication? Communication is essential during every step of the process.

- *Frequently communicate the plan and expectations for the organization.*
- *Communicate how well the company is performing, the good and the bad, and don't sugar coat it; tell the score.*
- *Communicate learnings. Never let a bad situation go the waste.*
- *Communicate actions taken to improve performance and the system.*
- *Recognize good performance.*
- *Communicate in different ways and say it 10 times.*

## Summarizing the Goal ZERO Roadmap

I "reverse engineered" the 10 Step Goal ZERO Roadmap for Operational Excellence by looking back at the progress we made throughout my career. I did my best to recreate and clean up the actions and steps we took. We didn't have a roadmap like this one to guide us and, in writing the book, I felt such a roadmap would be useful. We had many false starts and numerous discussions along the way. Everyone had diverse opinions and collectively we came up with a better work product than any of us could have developed on our own. And, most importantly, the work product developed transformative results.

As I mentioned, if you already have a management system, you can use this roadmap as a guide to enhance your system, especially simplifying your system documents and increasing the accountability, efficiency, and contributions of your technical organization.

Achieving Operational Excellence isn't easy. You must have a clear vision, determination, persistence, and constancy of purpose. However, once you achieve true Operational Excellence, it's a beautiful experience and its sustainable. It's the culmination of many, many small details of doing things the right way, every time.

# CHAPTER 10

## A Comprehensive Approach to Improvement

I began writing this book to share the experiences and learnings from my career. The book is a compilation of successful practices pulled together into a comprehensive approach to driving improvement. The applicable audience is very broad— from new people on up to CEOs. Throughout the writing process, I performed deeper research into several of the topics and learned a lot of additional information I wish I had learned much earlier in my career. I've captured those new learnings throughout the book.

I've always felt that if I could take away one or two learnings from a book, then buying and reading it was worthwhile. My wish is that each of you will have gathered at least a few tips in the book that will help you in your career and make your company better. You should be able to achieve improved reliability, quality, cost control, environmental performance, enhanced customer satisfaction, and improved safety; and, most importantly, you will continually protect people and save lives.

I was blessed to have a unique career: leading operations for the first half and leading global EH&S and Operational Excellence during the second half. I found that the actions required for good safety performance applied to everything else: product quality, reliability, cost control, people leadership, and on and on. Leading with a focus on safety makes sense to everyone and drives progress on Operational Excellence which in turn leads to business value creation.

I've explained how everything falls under the leadership, people, culture, systems, and assets umbrella. People can understand this formula and it provides a balanced approach for improvement. But make no mistake about it, everything begins with strong leadership. You, too, can be a results focused leader. Any organization can have assets and management systems, but the differentiator is how well people execute and deliver excellence. Superior leadership knows and understands how to attract, develop, inspire, and motivate their people. Creating pride in the organization and an attitude of winning will deliver best in class results. Leaders must have a compelling vision, create a winning culture, provide the resources needed for success and drive progress through a well-established management system.

I hope you understand by now that I'm a strong advocate of consistent terminology and consistency of purpose as W. Edwards Deming used to say. I like to choose consistent terminology and "elevator speech" messaging and then repeat the messages over and over. It takes time in an organization for people to understand the message you are trying to deliver. Stay away from programs of the month and be consistent over the long haul. That's the way to build a Goal ZERO culture.

Goal ZERO is so simple and yet so powerful. Goal ZERO establishes a very clear expectation for the kind of performance you expect, and it applies to all areas of your organization as well as each individual. It's a concept that says we expect ZERO defects, ZERO incidents, ZERO rule breaking, ZERO noncompliance, ZERO quality incidents, ZERO injuries, and ZERO missed opportunities that create significant value. In other words, employees should strive for perfection recognizing they will hit excellence along the way.

I discussed the importance that results focused leaders place on an Operational Excellence Management System. The management system is equivalent to the bare wood when you are doing a home remodeling job; you need something foundational upon which to build. A good functioning management system that is updated continually and followed consistently will assure that you never have to "go back to the basics" again.

I covered the importance of developing Excellence Models. Excellence Models contain documented best practices for a particular topic that are continually updated. A good Operational Excellence software system enables the continuous improvement process and communication to the appropriate people.

Excellence Model owners should be carefully selected and their performance monitored. No longer are these roles just filled with subject matter experts who respond to problems.

These individuals must have the skills and abilities to document and communicate their information in a clear and concise manner understandable to others. The Global Excellence Model framework provides excellent growth opportunities for technical professional individuals.

The Goal ZERO Roadmap for achieving Operational Excellence can be utilized no matter the condition of your current management system. The Roadmap works for all types of organizations—both manufacturing and service providers. Achieving Operational Excellence is a lot of work, but if you are serious about establishing a long-term sustainable system, this roadmap works.

Simplicity is a prevailing theme throughout the book. Most things are too complicated and need to be simplified. Simplicity applies to work processes, procedures, standards, guidance documents and so many other concepts. Remember, if you can't explain it simply, then you don't understand it well enough. And remember the quote, "I didn't have time to write you a short letter, so I wrote you a long one instead." Take the time to write your documents the right way and use the Flesch Reading Ease Score method to measure your results.

Finally, communication is such an important part of being an outstanding leader. The people in your organization and other stakeholders want to know what's going on and you must keep them updated. Leaders who are highly visible in the workplace are most effective, talking with and listening to their people. People appreciate knowing that you care about them, their welfare and what they do each day. People are most motivated when they are future focused and fully understand the direction of the company and its objectives. You must fine tune your communication skills in the various communication modes such as person to person, group settings, email, social media, newsletters, videos, etc. Never leave your people in the dark, especially during challenging times.

Throughout this book I talked about the importance of humility. I have suggested ways to achieve Operational Excellence, but absolutely there is more than one way. You may disagree with some of the concepts I've described and that's okay; diversity of thought is good. Work hard, do your best, be proud of your progress, but never be satisfied with how well you are doing. Take your work seriously but not yourself. Enjoy your life and remain balanced; remember the Seven Fs. If you have a good succession planning process in your company, the company will be just fine after you leave. You only live once, but if you do it right, once is enough.

As I end this book, I'd like to share a poem I enjoy that puts everything into perspective.

### "Indispensable Man"
**by Saxon White Kessinger**

*Sometime when you're feeling important;*
*Sometime when your ego's in bloom*
*Sometime when you take it for granted*
*You're the best qualified in the room,*

*Sometime when you feel that your going*
*Would leave an unfillable hole,*
*Just follow these simple instructions*
*And see how they humble your soul;*

*Take a bucket and fill it with water,*
*Put your hand in it up to the wrist,*
*Pull it out and the hole that's remaining*
*Is a measure of how you'll be missed.*

*You can splash all you wish when you enter,*
*You may stir up the water galore,*
*But stop and you'll find that in no time*
*It looks quite the same as before.*

*The moral of this quaint example*
*Is to just be the best that you can,*
*Be proud of yourself but remember,*
*There's no indispensable man.*

In closing, I have enjoyed writing this book more than I ever imagined. Like they say, writing the book was a labor of love and it took many, many hours to write—but it's been rewarding. *If you've benefited, I would be honored if you would take a moment to write a short review on Amazon.com. I normally wouldn't make such a request, but Amazon uses these comments to determine which books they should promote.* It's easy to do and I would appreciate it very much. Your review helps spread the word to others for improvement in their safety and overall performance.

All the best to you in your Goal ZERO journey towards excellence, superior performance and protecting your people!

# Goal ZERO Nuggets

# About the Author

As I look back, my values were heavily shaped by my parents, my faith, the Boy Scouts, and my competitive spirit from playing sports. Values are embedded in each of us at a very early stage in our lives.

Our childhood shapes who we become. I grew up in the very small town of Newgulf, Texas. Newgulf was a company town of around 1,000 people with all of the houses owned by the company, Texasgulf Sulphur Company. The Newgulf site was the largest sulphur-producing dome in the world with up to 15,000 tons of sulphur produced and shipped each day.

We had six children in our family; I was the oldest and had five younger, wonderful sisters—Lou Ann, Gayle, Jackie, Gina, and Lisa. I believe being the oldest of six children taught me a sense of responsibility that lasted my entire life. We had, and still have, a loving and close family and growing up in Newgulf was wonderful.

We had enough money for the basics, but that was about it. The town was loaded with pecan trees, so we picked pecans every fall to earn spending money. We looked for discarded soft drink bottles to cash them in for 2 cents each. I looked for work at every opportunity—putting circulars on doors from the local grocery store, mowing yards, washing cars, preparing the Little League baseball field prior to games, and hauling thousands of bales of hay each summer.

My dad was an athlete. He was fast; in fact, he won the Texas state championship in hurdles in high school and went on to star as a running back at Wharton County Junior College and North Texas State, now called University of North Texas. In adult life, his entire focus was on raising his family. He and I spent a lot of time hunting and fishing. This time together developed my great love for conservation and the outdoors. He also devoted his time to coaching our Little League baseball teams and as a Boy Scout leader. He was highly competitive and expected us to be the best at all times and to win.

My mother was loving and instilled unconditional love in each of us. She was smart and was always there with a smiling face, helping and encouraging us. I miss them both and will forever be grateful for their guidance and support throughout my life.

I believe parents have the most influence over their children until around 12 years of age. Children's values, attitudes, and behaviors are largely established by then and parenting becomes more of coaching and persuasion after that. So, parents, begin from day one and make the most of those first 12 years.

My parents encouraged us to participate in as many activities as we could manage. Participation in multiple activities was easier back in those days growing up in a small town and attending a small school. Our parents expected us to make top grades in school and to always do our best. One incentive was free baseball tickets provided by the Houston Astros if you made straight A's the entire school year.

We were fortunate in Newgulf to have a youth golf organization with the clever name, "Divot Diggers." One of the local men, Harry Norrell, had a passion for youth and ran the club. Mr. Norrell spent a lot of personal time and energy helping us to learn the finer aspects of golf. One principle he instilled was attention to detail even when practicing—make every swing count. Treat each putt during practice just as important as the final putt of a tournament. My claim to fame in golf was playing in the same Texas High School State Championship Tournament as Ben Crenshaw (although we never met each other).

Another principle Mr. Norrell taught was being able to **remain calm** during competition and adversity. He taught this lesson by constantly creating a competitive environment. After school, we would have small contests for putting, chipping, driving, or any aspect of the game. The prize was typically a hamburger or a shake at the local cafe which was a real treat for us. His real objective was to treat practice the same as a competitive event and this experience served us well for the many tournaments in which we participated.

I loved my Boy Scout Days and proudly earned the rank of Eagle Scout. I progressed into leadership positions from a very early age. In Boy Scouts, I achieved Patrol Leader and then Senior Patrol Leader of the troop. I was pitcher on our baseball teams, quarterback on our high school football team, and held numerous officer positions in high school and college organizations. I became fascinated with the concepts of leadership, excellence, and how to get the best out of people. This fascination has remained with me throughout my life.

I paid my own way through college by earning scholarships, working summer and part-time jobs, and taking out a modest student loan which I paid back over the next 10 years. I received a Bachelor of Science degree in Chemical Engineering at The University of Texas. I had terrific friends in college, and we were all in a similar situation, with not much extra spending money. On spring break, for example, we never even thought about going to Cancun or any other hot spot. We were out hustling some work to make a little extra spending money. In the long run, we all look back and know that it didn't hurt us. In fact, this experience helped shape our behaviors and work ethics for the rest of our lives.

I've always had a strong sense of curiosity in what motivates people and how to make things better. I tend to face problems in a positive manner, not only addressing the problem at hand but naturally focusing on how to make improvements. In a strange way, I see difficulties as an opportunity to get better.

My colleagues have described me as being extremely persistent. It's true—I don't give up easily. Driving change takes persistence since most people are resistant to change. If you believe strongly in something or have a clear vision of what needs to be done, never give up.

I loved the people I worked with and always tried to show the same respect for our cleaning staff as I would for any top-level executive (the cleaning staff employees were actually a lot more fun). Every person tries to do his or her best and I always appreciated that fact. Although I relocated a few times, I still remember the people I worked with at each location and the contributions they made to our success. I have long lasting friends in many countries around the world that I can call tomorrow for help or just to have a friendly conservation.

I had a relatively unique career. The first half consisted of research and manufacturing plant leadership roles. I was able to obtain one United States patent. I had a reputation for improving a plant's operation and the morale of the workforce. As a result, I was "rewarded" by being sent to a number of manufacturing plants with significant problems. These plants required a lot of hard work, but in the end, these experiences prepared me well.

During the last 20 years of my career, I was given the opportunity by the companies I worked for to lead the global Environment, Safety, Health, Security, Operational Excellence, and Sustainable Development functions. Leading these global functions was a major change for me. Driving performance improvement for tens of thousands of individuals in countries all over the world was a huge challenge.

On the other hand, I found it easy since I had been in the shoes of the many people that I was now expected to influence. It was the first opportunity in which I had the time to focus on the finer aspects of human behavior, organizational efficiency, the power of management systems, and working through influence of others to drive improvement. I found it extremely rewarding to set ambitious goals, provide leadership, create the system, and observe a paradigm shift in performance that we expected from our people around the world. The most gratifying aspect was the number of injuries we prevented around the world and the lives we potentially saved.

During each of my assignments, I had a passion for learning and for leadership. Throughout the years, I worked to capture these learnings and build on them with each successive assignment. The companies that I worked for included:

- *Summer jobs with Texasgulf Sulphur Company, Atlantic Richfield (ARCO) and Exxon*
- *The Dow Chemical Company*
  - *Research, Manufacturing, and Global Vice President—Environment, Health, Safety, Security and Sustainable Development*
- *Royal Dutch Shell*
  - *Global Vice President—Downstream Environment, Health, Safety, and Sustainable Development*
- *LyondellBasell Industries*
  - *Senior Vice President—Americas Manufacturing, and Global Vice President—Environment, Health, Safety, Security, and Operational Excellence*

Since my retirement, I have been as busy as ever enjoying life and creating *Flow*. People that retire to the rocking chair don't rock very long. I remain faithful to God and what comes next. I love hanging out with my family and friends and spending a lot of time in the outdoors. Staying in good shape is a priority. Having fun is always high on the list. I serve on one public and one private company board of directors and spend a lot of time with Ducks Unlimited, the world's leader in wetlands and waterfowl conservation. I serve on the Dean's Engineering Advisory Board at The University of Texas. Balance is key and the Seven Fs apply consistently.

# Bibliography

1. Belitz, Justin. *Success: Full Living.* Knowledge Systems, 1991.

2. Csikszentmihalyi, Mihaly. *Flow - The Psychology of Optimal Experience.* New York: Harper & Row Publishers, 1990.

3. Daniels, Aubrey C. *Bringing Out the Best in People: How to Apply the Astonishing Power of Positive Reinforcement.* New York: McGraw Hill, 1994.

4. Deming, W. Edwards. *Out of the Crisis.* Cambridge, Massachusetts: Massachusetts Institute of Technology, Center for Advanced Engineering Study, 1982.

5. Denny, Richard. *Motivate to Win: How to Motivate Yourself and Others to Really Get Results.* Kogan Page, 2009.

6. Flesch, Rudolph F. *How to Write in Plain English: A Book for Lawyers and Consumers.* New York: Barnes and Noble Books, 1979.

7. Gray, William S. and Leary, Bernice E. *What Makes a Book Readable.* Chicago: The University of Chicago Press, 1935.

8. Jensen, Bill. *Simplicity: The New Competitive Advantage in a World of More, Better, Faster.* Cambridge, Massachusetts: Perseus Publishing, 2000.

9. Klare, George R. and Buck, Byron. *Know Your Reader: The Scientific Approach to Readability.* New York: Hermitage House, 1954.

10. Kincaid, J.P., Fishburne, R.P., Rogers, R.L., & Chissom, B.S. *Derivation of new readability formulas (automated readability index, fog count, and Flesch reading ease formula) for Navy enlisted personnel.* Research Branch Report 8-75. Chief of Naval Technical Training: Naval Air Station Memphis. 1975.

11. LyondellBasell. *Operational Excellence Management System Expectations.* March 2015.

12. Martin, Roger L. *M&A: The One Thing You Need to Get Right.* Harvard Business Review, June 2016.

13. Michaels, Dr. David. *7 Ways to Improve Operations Without Sacrificing Safety.* Harvard Business Review, March 21, 2018.

14. Piasecki, Bruce. *Doing More with Teams: The New Way to Winning.* New York: Square One Publishers, 2016.

15. Spear, Steven J. *The High Velocity Edge: How Market Leaders Leverage Operational Experience to Beat the Competition.* New York: McGraw Hill Education, 2009.

# Index

# Full Endorsements

"I wish *The Power of Goal ZERO* had been available and part of the required reading list when I was in business school. It doesn't matter if you are just starting your career or if you are a CEO, Sam Smolik's book is a must read. It clearly illustrates how to achieve Operational Excellence, which should be the ultimate goal of any business or organization."
**– Rogers Hoyt, Jr., Chairman of the Board, Ducks Unlimited, Inc.**

"In his humble, unique way, Sam has turned a lifetime of learning into a must-read book on the essence of common sense in leadership. He has taken a subject many take for granted and provided a clear roadmap for current and future leaders to achieve Operational Excellence. His passion for leading people leaps off the page and is a powerful, contagious lesson. Thanks Sam, for reminding us that Goal ZERO is achievable through motivating people to perform at their best."
**— Chet Thompson, President & CEO, American Fuel & Petrochemical Manufacturers (AFPM)**

"Built on his experience as a successful senior operations executive and influential board member, Sam Smolik's practical advice on leadership and driving outstanding business performance is an invaluable guide for executives of all levels and industries. This book is a must read for anyone seeking to take his/her organization to the next level of performance and competitive differentiation!"
**— Robert W. Bryant, Chief Executive Officer, Axalta Coating Systems**

"*The Power of Goal ZERO* is a must-read for any CEO seeking a shift change in his/her company performance. It guides readers step by step through the delicate journey to Excellence. It reads like a novel and speaks to safety practitioners in very clear and straightforward terms. This Opus demonstrates Smolik's lifetime commitment to the industry and unveils an inspiring legacy to the young generation of Leaders for Excellence. Hats off, Sam. Job well done!"
**— William Garcia, Executive Director, Cefic, The European Chemicals Industry Council**

"Sam Smolik's decades of experience in high hazard industries and his passion for safety led him to write this book about Goal ZERO. Safety is about culture, people, and a focus on embedding it as a core value. Sam's approach is to make this book a must read for anyone who wants a roadmap to safety excellence."
— **Katie Mehnert, Chief Executive Officer, ALLY Energy**

"Sam's passion for safety really comes through in this book. Safety performance is about leadership, culture, processes, and discipline. This book is a very practical guide for achieving safety excellence."
— **Bob Patel, Chief Executive Officer, Lyondellbasell Industries**

"Having the privilege of knowing Sam for over forty years, not only working for him early in our careers but later having him serve on one of my public company boards, I can attest to the power of his Goal Zero design and execution in improving business performance. His book accomplishes what hundreds of other publications have attempted to do, which is to simplify and clearly state how to achieve step change in an organization. Sam's clear articulation and toolbox for business improvement is not limited to operations but applies to any functional or commercial improvement effort undertaken. This is an excellent read for not only senior leaders in an organization but also for mid and entry level personnel looking for ways to affect change with positive results."
— **Charlie Shaver, Chairman and CEO, Nouryon Chemicals (Carlyle Private Equity)**

"The benefits of powerful storytelling in business are clear. In his book, *The Power of Goal ZERO*, Sam Smolik offers a clear and comprehensive guide for any business leader who wants to operate a highly successful organization. *The Power of Goal ZERO* will help you gain an edge on your competition, grow your brand, and most importantly, develop a more loyal, engaged workforce. *The Power of Goal ZERO* offers valuable lessons for business majors who want to launch, manage, or work in successful companies; therefore, I believe it should be required reading in business schools around the country."
— **Marianne Gooch, President, DynaComm**

"Sam Smolik was my very first management new hire at LyondellBasell after I was brought in to help the company recover and emerge from bankruptcy. The stunning turnaround at LyondellBasell post-bankruptcy emergence was first and foremost a plant floor revolution. Our employees led the way with best-in-class operational performance, cost structure and most importantly, industry leading safety results. Those wearing hard hats and coveralls to work were the heroes of the greatest corporate turnaround of all time and Sam and I were among their cheerleaders."
— James Gallogly, Former Chief Executive Officer, LyondellBasell

"Sam Smolik is the ideal author of this definitive book on Goal ZERO. He combines senior leadership experience at three global Energy/Chemical companies with a clear, concise writing style. His book is destined to be a best seller on this topic. I highly recommend our clients use Sam's wisdom in how they lead."
— George Pilko, Founder and Chairman, Pilko & Associates

"Sam Smolik is a true industry leader with a lot of proven success. His companies have prospered by achieving Excellence. *The Power of Goal ZERO* is strong because it is real event driven with truthful outcomes."
— Jon Hodges, Founder and CEO, Evergreen North America

"So much of business literature is theoretical and untested. When you invest 50 years of your life into something with the passion and skill of Sam Smolik, amazing things happen. Businesses have been improved and transformed, people have been changed, and most importantly, through his focus on safety, lives have been saved. I am grateful that he took the time to document this for the rest of us, allowing his impact to continue. Very well done!"
— Kevin Garland, Chief Executive Officer, Mountaire Farms

"Sam Smolik has had a distinguished career and has always been a champion of Operational Excellence. Sam has done an outstanding job of capturing the lessons learned as well as best practices, not only from his own experience, but also from others in the industry. This book offers a comprehensive step-by-step approach to creating an incident and injury free

workplace. The principles can also be applied to improve business performance in any area. A must read for today's managers."
— **Jeet Bindra, Retired President, Chevron Global Manufacturing**

"*The Power of Goal ZERO* challenges all organizations to raise operational performance expectations and provides a roadmap/framework to meet these high-performance aspirations—no injuries, no defects, no missed opportunities. It highlights the powerful levers of strong foundational values, clear and consistent communication, and organization-wide involvement/ownership. The book is a "toolbox" of ideas (drawn from Sam's personal experiences) on how to fully support and bring out the best in team members. Leaders at all levels can benefit from Sam's experiences and suggestions here."
— **Phil Hawk, former Chairman and Chief Executive Officer, TEAM, Inc.**

"Having spent a couple decades behind the curtain at the enterprise-level with some of the world's most advanced Operational Excellence—driven companies (e.g., Chevron, ExxonMobil, LyondellBasell, etc.), I am comfortable concluding that Sam's book is the most comprehensive on the topic— from the tactics and anecdotes for leaders to the strategies and philosophies behind the best Operational Excellence Management Systems in industry today."
— **Joe Stough, Founder and Former Chief Executive Officer of Syntex**

"To read this book is to know Sam Smolik—honest, open, straightforward, and sincere who cares for and enjoys people. As a close friend for over 60 years, I believe I'm qualified to offer this insight on the man. Sam has always been a leader, but a leader that made others feel like they were. In this book Sam carefully lays out his experiences and path to Operational Excellence using Goal ZERO in a manner, which to repeat his words, "is easy to understand." His story telling technique is backed by hard guidance and real examples to cover complex topics in a way that the reader can enjoy and perhaps absorb. For many readers, this is an opportunity to benefit from an industry executive that you never had the chance to interview."
— **David Zimmerman, PE and Former Group President, KBR, Inc.**

"Informed by an almost 50-year career of leadership experience with some of the world's most recognized and admired manufacturing companies, Sam has captured the essence of how strong and empathetic leadership can drive sustainable business performance to the highest levels. This book provides a rigorous yet practical approach that has relevance whether you are an emerging EHS&S or manufacturing leader, a veteran functional leader seeking to refine his/her skills or a CEO who is committed to profound change. Sam's blend of strategic intent with real world examples of successes and failures makes for a compelling and inspiring read. Sam gets it!"
— **Don A. Young, Executive Vice President of EHS & Sustainability, J.M. Huber Corporation**

"It was a privilege for me to work with Sam and contribute to the step change in LyondellBasell's safety performance. He brought leadership and drive to LyondellBasell and changed our safety culture and mindset. Goal ZERO became, and still is, our safety motto. It is part of our daily vocabulary and ZERO will be reached in occupational safety, process safety and environment thanks to what Sam brought to LyondellBasell. His book will help you discover your journey to Goal ZERO. Enjoy!"
— **Jean Gadbois, Senior Vice President Manufacturing Europe, Asia, and International, LyondellBasell**

"Sam knows his stuff. Through his leadership at some of the safest companies in the world, he has reduced risk, saved lives, and driven Operational Excellence. This book describes how to apply the highly successful Goal ZERO approach to both safety and Operational Excellence, all wrapped up in a management system. This book is based on sound theory and practical implementation. A must read for leaders committed to world-class performance!"
— **Laurence Pearlman, Senior Vice President, Consulting Solutions, Marsh Advisory**

"By collecting decades of experiences in his book, *The Power of Goal ZERO*, Sam Smolik created the definitive blueprint for manufacturing excellence. It simplifies the complexities of operating discipline into a step-by-step instruction manual that both the newest and most seasoned professionals can

immediately use. Sam's fun stories, simple wisdoms, and insightful perspective will change the way you think, improve your organization's performance, and is a book that every new engineer should read on Day One of his/her career."
— **Dustin Olson, Chief Manufacturing Officer, Purecycle Technologies**

"I witnessed first-hand *The Power of Goal ZERO* when I went to work for Sam. Goal ZERO is about a complete culture shift in the beliefs workers have regarding how to take the best and safest actions to become excellent in everything they do. The change was remarkable; over time an observable culture shift had taken place. As a Safety & Health professional, the Goal ZERO transformation was one of the most exciting and rewarding experiences of my career."
— **Cynthia Childs, CSP/CIH (retired), Former Americas HSE Director, LyondellBasell**

"I had the privilege of working with Sam during my global road safety role in Shell International and contributing to the Goal ZERO journey in road safety. Thinking outside the box, challenging the routine, striving to continuously improve, and leading from the front are hallmarks of Sam Smolik. Add to this a unique ability to motivate thousands of staff across all continents and a perfect team player—that is the Sam I knew. In my 40+ years of industrial experience, I always felt that there is vast gap between academic's style of teaching and industry requirements particularly in logistics and Operational Excellence fields. With writing this valuable book, Sam has bridged this yawning gap. A must read for all managers who want to achieve lasting success in their operations."
— **Ashok Kulkarni, Former Road Safety Manager—Asia, Africa, Middle East & Oceania, Shell International**

"Sam Smolik has taken a lifetime of experiences and crafted a toolbox for leaders and aspiring leaders who have the courage to grab the tools, follow the blueprint and transform the effectiveness and efficiency of their organizations. This book will charm you with its style, capture you with its numerous examples and guide you on a pathway to a better tomorrow. Take a well-deserved break, sit down, and enjoy a challenging read. You'll be glad you did."
— **Alex Pollock, Equipping You LLC**

"Sam's Goal Zero approach enables teams and organizations to translate their business aspirations into individual and collective actions which very quickly bring tangible improvements. On a personal level, Sam's leadership was second to none and he had the rare ability to take you on a journey with him—you were determined to play your part in making a positive contribution. I highly recommend his Goal ZERO strategy and related actions for making a step-change in any company's organizational effectiveness."
— **Tim Wotton, Head of Communications, Peninsula Petroleum, London**

"This book should be required reading for anyone in operations or EH&S roles, as it will accelerate their understanding of both the systems and the behaviors required to drive improvement. Not only does *The Power of Goal ZERO* clearly describe the mindset required and the justification for setting a goal of zero for undesirable events, but the book also provides a road map to take the necessary steps to get there."
— **Mike McCandless, Managing Director—Operational Excellence/Risk Management, Pilko & Associates**

Lightning Source UK Ltd.
Milton Keynes UK
UKHW011329180621
385747UK00009B/584/J